State and Federal
Regulation
of National Advertising

AEI STUDIES IN REGULATION AND FEDERALISM
Christopher C. DeMuth and Jonathan R. Macey, series editors

COSTLY POLICIES: STATE REGULATION AND ANTITRUST EXEMPTION
IN INSURANCE MARKETS
Jonathan R. Macey and Geoffrey P. Miller

FEDERALISM IN TAXATION: THE CASE FOR GREATER UNIFORMITY
Daniel Shaviro

PRODUCT-RISK LABELING: A FEDERAL RESPONSIBILITY
W. Kip Viscusi

STATE AND FEDERAL REGULATION OF NATIONAL ADVERTISING
J. Howard Beales and Timothy J. Muris

State and Federal Regulation of National Advertising

J. Howard Beales and Timothy J. Muris

The AEI Press

Publisher for the American Enterprise Institute
WASHINGTON, D.C.

1993

Distributed by arrangement with

University Press of America, Inc.
4720 Boston Way   3 Henrietta Street
Lanham, Md. 20706   London WC2E 8LU England

Library of Congress Cataloging-in-Publication Data

Beales, J. Howard.
    State and Federal regulation of national advertising / J. Howard
Beales and Timothy J. Muris.
        p.   cm.
    ISBN 0-8447-3825-5 (cloth).—ISBN 0-8447-3824-7 (paper)
    1. Advertising laws—United States.   I. Muris, Timothy J.
II. Title.
KF1614.B4   1992
343.73'082—dc20
[347.30382]   92-38187
                                                                  CIP

1 3 5 7 9 10 8 6 4 2

THE AEI PRESS
Publisher for the American Enterprise Institute
1150 Seventeenth Street, N.W., Washington, D.C. 20036

Printed in the United States of America

Contents

93-H270

CONTENTS

vi

Foreword

J. HOWARD BEALES AND TIMOTHY J. MURIS'S study of state and federal regulation of national advertising is one of a series of research monographs commissioned by the American Enterprise Institute's Regulation and Federalism Project. The purpose of the project is to examine the advantages and disadvantages of American federalism in important areas of contemporary business regulation, including product labeling, insurance, transportation, taxation, communications, and environmental quality.

The benefits of state autonomy—diversity, responsiveness to local circumstances, and constraint on the power of the national government—are fundamental to the American political creed and deeply embedded in our political institutions. Are these benefits real and substantial in the case of business regulation? How do they compare with the costs of duplication, inconsistency, and interference with free interstate commerce that state regulation can entail? Has the growth of national and international commerce altered the balance of federalism's benefits and costs—for example, by affecting the ability of individual states to pursue local policies at the expense of citizens of other states? Are there practical means of reducing the economic costs of state autonomy in regulation while preserving its political benefits?

The authors of these volumes have found different answers to these questions in the context of different markets and regulatory regimes: they call for greater national uniformity in some cases, greater state autonomy in others, and a revision of the rules of state "policy competition" in still others. We hope that this research will be useful to officials and legislators at all levels of government and to the business executives who must live with their policies. More generally, we hope that the AEI project will prove to be a significant contribution to our understanding of one of the most distinctive and important features of American government.

Each of the monographs produced for the Regulation and Federalism Project was discussed and criticized at an AEI seminar involving federal and state lawmakers, business executives, professionals, and academic experts with a wide range of interests and viewpoints. I would like to thank all of them for their contributions, noting, however, that final exposition and conclusions were entirely the work of the authors of each monograph. I am particularly grateful to Jonathan R. Macey of Cornell University and Heather Gradison of AEI, who organized and directed the project's research and seminars along with me, and to John D. Ong and Jon V. Heider of the BFGoodrich Company and Patricia H. Engman of The Business Roundtable, who suggested the project in the first place, worked hard and effectively to raise financial support for it, and provided valuable counsel and encouragement throughout.

CHRISTOPHER C. DeMUTH
President, American Enterprise Institute
for Public Policy Research

Acknowledgments

THE AUTHORS thank Nicole Verrier and Donna Walker for their valuable assistance and, for their numerous comments and suggestions, Jon Macey, Paul Pauter, Bill MacLeod, and participants at workshops at AEI and the George Mason University School of Law. The authors have greatly benefited from prior experience regarding advertising, including health and environmental claims, within the government and as consultants for private clients.

About the Authors

J. Howard Beales III is associate professor of strategic management and public policy at the George Washington University School of Business and Public Management. His numerous articles on the economics of information and its application to consumer protection problems have appeared in the *Journal of Public Policy and Marketing*, the *Journal of Law and Economics*, the *Journal of Consumer Research*, and the *Journal of Marketing*. Mr. Beales has served as branch chief in the Office of Management and Budget's Office of Information and Regulatory Affairs, overseeing FDA regulations. He received his B.A. magna cum laude from Georgetown University in 1972, and his Ph.D. in economics from the University of Chicago in 1978.

Timothy J. Muris is Foundation Professor of Law at George Mason University. He has published numerous articles concerning antitrust, consumer protection, government regulation of business, and the organization of business activity. He was formerly director of the Federal Trade Commission's Bureau of Consumer Protection and director of the Bureau of Competition, as well as executive associate director of the Office of Management and Budget, and deputy counsel to President Reagan's Task Force on Regulatory Relief.

State and Federal Regulation of National Advertising

1
Introduction

To SELL THEIR PRODUCTS, businesses must communicate with consumers. Although the most visible form of communication is advertising through the electronic or print media, communication also occurs at the point of sale, both through display materials and through information on the product's label. Historically, for firms that sell products across state boundaries, advertising campaigns were regulated, with minor exceptions, only at the federal level. Since the mid-1980s, some state attorneys general have aggressively pursued certain categories of national advertising. Because of the states' involvement, national advertisers have increasingly faced conflicting state and federal standards.

Health and environmental claims have been focal points of the tension between state and federal regulation. As Americans became more health-conscious and as scientific evidence grew about the links between diet and health, many businesses turned to advertising based on health characteristics. In the late 1980s, with growing concern over the environmental consequences of waste disposal and other aspects of producing, consuming, and disposing of consumer products, firms began to advertise environmental attributes of their products. State and federal regulators have carefully scrutinized both types of claims, trumpeting enforcement action aimed at reducing perceived fraud and deception.

Both areas have produced widespread calls for tough federal legislation and regulation. Consumer groups have supported federal action because of the allegedly high level of consumer misinformation and deception. Businesses have sought federal action to avoid the sometimes conflicting standards imposed by state and federal regulators—conflicts that can be exacerbated by the presence of two federal regulators, such as the Federal Trade Commission (FTC) and the Food and Drug Administration (FDA), regarding health claims.

1

Thus the regulation of national advertising presents a ripe opportunity to study the impact of coexisting state and federal regulation.

We divide this study into four parts. Because the subject matter of the regulation is advertising, a topic with a long and complex history in law enforcement, we begin with a discussion of the appropriate regulatory principles to apply to business communication with consumers. We focus on the Federal Trade Commission, the primary federal agency charged with regulating advertising. The FTC's accumulated experience has resulted in a major evolution of its approach to advertising. The hostility to advertising that once characterized the agency's decisions, particularly through the 1960s, has given way to an approach based on the belief that advertising, appropriately constrained, is a powerful tool for reducing consumer ignorance. Many states take the earlier approach of the Federal Trade Commission, demonstrating much more hostility toward advertising than the FTC has in the past twenty years. Throughout, we primarily use the health claims controversy, which has a longer history than that over environmental claims, to illustrate the differences.

With this background, part two examines the current status of the health and environmental claims controversies. We address the federal legislation regarding health claims on labels, legislation that in part attempts to resolve the controversy between the different approaches of state and federal regulators. Regarding environmental claims, we evaluate the conflict between the proposals of some states and the modern FTC approach toward advertising. Part three discusses the issue of advertising and federalism more generally, seeking appropriate principles for resolving federalism conflicts about advertising. To understand some of the sources of the tension between state and federal regulators, this part also addresses the bureaucratic constraints and incentives that face the different regulators. Finally, part four summarizes our conclusions, regarding both the results of the case studies and the more general topic of the appropriate regulation of national advertising.

PART ONE

How Should Advertising Be Regulated?

In almost every year since its creation in 1914, the Federal Trade Commission has scrutinized advertising for possible deception. Through the 1960s, the commission's underlying view of advertising was one of hostility, reflecting the view of many in the academic community. In the 1970s, economists increasingly came to recognize the importance of advertising in reducing consumer ignorance, and the commission's attitude toward advertising changed as well. Chapter 2 discusses how advertising is essential for the optimal functioning of a market economy and analyzes the conflicting views about advertising that have existed at the Federal Trade Commission, conflicts that are at the heart of the debates about health and environmental claims today. We will see that many states reflect the older FTC view about advertising— deep suspicion about the role of advertising in the economy—resulting in a regulatory scheme that finds "deception" to be widespread. The modern FTC, on the other hand, has abandoned this earlier view, recognizing that consumers can be seriously harmed when standards are too restrictive.

The next two chapters analyze two of the most important issues in determining the proper regulatory regime. Chapter 3 discusses the interpretation problem—that is, how to address the question of what an ad means. Chapter 4, "The Problem of Too Much Information," considers how the desire of many regulators to require extensive disclosures in advertising causes more harm than good.

Many of the examples in this part involve health claims. A growing number of scientific studies have demonstrated the link between diet and disease. One hears increasingly, for example, of the dangers of cholesterol and saturated fats, as well as the benefits of fiber. As evidence of the importance of diet has grown, government regulators, academics, public health advocates, and others have increased their efforts to educate the public. Commercial entities, motivated undoubt-

5

edly by a desire for profit, have also increased their efforts to communicate the link between nutrition and health, and to urge that their products be part of a total diet. Most notably, in late 1984 Kellogg began advertising and adding labels that cited the National Cancer Institute's (NCI) statements about the link between consumption of fiber-rich foods and cancer. Other companies quickly promoted the fiber content of their products and, in some instances, the health benefits relating to fiber. Although the original Kellogg campaign was a cooperative effort with the NCI, government agencies have not preapproved most health claims.

The use of health claims in promoting products has caused much concern among government regulators. All have recognized that laissez faire is inadequate. Consumers cannot evaluate accurately the truthfulness of such claims, giving unscrupulous firms an incentive to deceive the public. There has been considerable debate, however, regarding the appropriate standards to apply to health claims. Some, particularly at the FDA and in several states that have used health claims to launch vigorous scrutiny of national advertising, would ban or severely restrict such claims. Others, most notably at the Federal Trade Commission, would allow health claims to be made if they fall within the commission's long-standing substantiation program—that is, if they are supported by a "reasonable basis." These approaches produce very different results.

2
Advertising and the Law

OVER THE PAST FEW DECADES, the FTC has come to recognize the competitive importance of advertising, both as a spur to effective price competition and as an aid in developing products that best satisfy consumer demands. Indeed, a consensus has emerged that restrictions on truthful advertising harm consumers. This consensus is reflected in the commission's movement away from cases that primarily protect competitors from vigorous competition, and toward actions that enhance the ability of advertising to provide information for consumers. We first discuss the reason behind the FTC's change in policy—namely, recognition of the economic importance of advertising. We then briefly summarize the FTC's approach before 1970. Finally we discuss the changes in the FTC's approach, and how some states still follow the earlier FTC rules. This chapter will introduce the divergence in views regarding the regulation of advertising. The following chapters will provide greater detail.

The Economic Importance of Advertising

Scholars have long studied whether advertising creates artificial product differentiation to enhance the monopoly power of leading firms or whether it facilitates entry of new producers and new products, thereby encouraging competition and benefiting consumers. Since Nobel laureate George Stigler's 1961 article on the economics of information, economists have increasingly come to recognize that, because it reduces the costs of obtaining information, advertising enhances economic performance.[1] As Stigler noted, it is "an immensely powerful instrument for the elimination of ignorance."[2] In a competitive economy, consumer choices guide produc-

---

[1]George Stigler, "The Economics of Information," *Journal of Political Economy*, vol. 64 (1961), p. 213.

[2]Ibid., p. 220.

ers' decisions about what and how much to produce. In turn, what consumers know about competing alternatives influences their choices. Better information about the options enables consumers to make choices that better serve their interests.

Information, however, is costly. The costs may sometimes be monetary, as in the case of a subscription to *Consumer Reports* or another magazine that offers product reviews. Moreover, obtaining and using information always takes time and effort—to find relevant information, to read it, and to understand its implications. Because information is costly, consumers do not seek complete knowledge. Instead they balance the potential gains (in the form of better choices) from additional information against the extra costs of obtaining more. Stigler's seminal insight was that advertising greatly reduces the costs of obtaining more information. Consumers therefore are better informed, resulting in enhanced market performance.

The clearest evidence of the importance of advertising in competitive markets comes from studies of the impact of state restrictions on advertising. An early study examined state prohibitions against advertising by optometrists, finding that prices were approximately 25 percent higher in states with such restrictions.[3] Moreover, prices in restrictive states seemed to be highest for the least educated consumers.[4] Numerous studies of advertising restrictions in a variety of other industries—legal services, prescription drugs, gasoline price posting, and cigarettes—found that restrictions on advertising increased prices.[5] Studies of the introduction of advertising for estab-

---

[3]Lee Benham, "The Effect of Advertising on the Price of Eyeglasses," *Journal of Law and Economics*, vol. 15 (1972), p. 337. An FTC study of a variety of other restrictions in the optometric market found similar results. See R. S. Bond, J. J. Kwoka, J. J. Phelan, and I. T. Whitten, *Effects of Restrictions on Advertising and Commercial Practice in the Professions: The Case of Optometry* (1980), FTC Bureau of Economics Staff Report.

[4]Lee Benham and Alexandra Benham, "Regulating through the Professions: A Perspective on Information Control," *Journal of Law and Economics*, vol. 18 (1975), p. 421.

[5]*Legal Services:* John R. Schroeter, Scott L. Smith, and Steven R. Cox, "Advertising and Competition in Routine Legal Service Markets: An Empirical Investigation," *Journal of Industrial Economics*, vol. 36 (1987), p. 49; William W. Jacobs, Brenda W. Doubrava, Robert P. Weaver, Douglas O. Stewart, and Eric L. Prahl, *Improving Consumer Access to Legal Services: The Case for Removing Restrictions on Truthful Advertising* (1984) (FTC Staff Report). *Gasoline:* Alex Maurizi and Thomas Kelley,

lished products also found that advertising significantly lowered prices, even when the advertising was primarily directed to children.[6]

Advertising is critical to competitive markets for another reason: it informs consumers about the availability of new products, new features, or new information about existing products. Such information is vital to the competitive process. Without the ability to inform consumers about a new or different alternative, the incentive to introduce new alternatives is reduced. For example, an FTC Bureau of Economics study discussed in detail below found that after the introduction of advertising claims discussing the relationship between fiber and cancer, the number and the fiber content of new product introductions in the cereal market increased. This led to greater weighted-average fiber content of cereals in the market.[7] Advertising is thus an extremely efficient way of providing consumers the products they desire. When even a minority of consumers is better informed about the options available, competition among sellers for the business of such consumers is more effective.[8] The result is lower prices and better products for all consumers.

The history of FTC policy toward cigarette advertising provides one of the clearest examples of the economic importance of advertising, as well as of the commission's evolving recognition of that importance. Concerned about growing competition between cigarette companies over filters and tar and nicotine content—satirically

---

Prices and Consumer Information: The Benefits from Posting Retail Gasoline Prices (Washington, D.C.: American Enterprise Institute, 1978). *Prescription Drugs:* J. F. Cady, *Restricted Advertising and Competition: The Case of Retail Drugs* (Washington, D.C.: American Enterprise Institute, 1976). *Cigarettes*, effect of broadcast ban: Robert H. Porter, "The Impact of Government Policy on the U.S. Cigarette Industry," in Pauline Ippolito and D. Scheffman, eds., *Empirical Approaches to Consumer Protection* (Washington, D.C.: Federal Trade Commission, March 1986).

[6]Robert L. Steiner, "Does Advertising Lower Consumer Prices?" *Journal of Marketing*, vol. 37 (1973), p. 19; toy advertising directed to children. Robert L. Steiner, "Learning from the Past—Brand Advertising and the Great Bicycle Craze of the 1890s," in *Advances in Advertising Research and Management* (1978).

[7]Pauline M. Ippolito and Alan D. Mathios, *Health Claims in Advertising and Labeling: A Study of the Cereal Market* (August 1989), FTC Bureau of Economics Staff Report (BE Fiber Study), pp. 42, 47.

[8]See J. Howard Beales, Richard Craswell & Steven C. Salop, "The Efficient Regulation of Consumer Information," *Journal of Law and Economics*, vol. 24 (1981), p. 491.

labeled the "tar derby"—the commission in 1960 reached an informal agreement with the cigarette companies to end all tar and nicotine claims and claims about comparative efficiency of filters. Because this agreement prevented cigarette manufacturers from describing important product attributes, it hindered the growth and development of cigarettes with lowered tar and nicotine content.[9] In the four years preceding the agreement, the sales-weighted average tar content of cigarettes fell 29 percent; in the four years after the ban, it declined only 16 percent.[10]

Faced with mounting criticism of its policy, the commission in 1966 announced that it would once again permit tar and nicotine advertising. In 1967 it developed a standardized test methodology for tar and nicotine content. In 1970 the commission proposed a rule to require disclosure of the very information it had prohibited ten years earlier. By 1981 the sales-weighted average tar content of cigarettes had fallen 39 percent from its 1968 level.[11]

Thus advertising regulation must consider the importance of advertising in maintaining a competitive marketplace. As former commissioner Robert Pitofsky noted:

> Protection of consumers against advertising fraud should not be a broad, theoretical effort to achieve Truth, but rather a practical enterprise to ensure the existence of reliable data which in turn will facilitate an efficient and reliable competitive market process.[12]

The FTC before 1970

In the 1950s and 1960s, the commission pursued numerous trivial cases with little appreciation of the importance of advertising in

---

[9]Robert McAuliffe, "The FTC and the Effectiveness of Cigarette Advertising Regulations," *Journal of Public Policy and Marketing*, vol. 7 (1988), pp. 49, 50.

[10]Data obtained from the Tobacco Institute. See also John Calfee, *Cigarette Advertising, Health Information and Regulation Before 1970* (December 1985), FTC Bureau of Economics Report.

[11]Federal Trade Commission, *Report to Congress Pursuant to the Federal Cigarette Labeling and Advertising Act for the Year 1981* (July 1984), table 12, p. 31.

[12]Robert Pitofsky, "Beyond Nader: Consumer Protection and the Regulation of Advertising," *Harvard Law Review*, vol. 90 (1977), pp. 661, 671.

enhancing competition. As the American Bar Association concluded in its 1969 report on the FTC,

> The FTC has tended to select relatively trivial practices for staunch enforcement measures . . . . the FTC has issued complaints attacking the failure to disclose on labels that "Navy shoes" were not made by the Navy, that [fishing] flies were imported, that Indian trinkets were not manufactured by American Indians, and that "Havana" cigars were not made entirely of Cuban tobacco. The record in relation to rules and guides also displays a preoccupation with projects of marginal importance. Thus the Commission announced that use of the word "automatic" is deceptive when used in relation to sewing machines because "sewing machines, unlike 'automatic' washing machines or dishwashers, cannot be turned on and left to operate by themselves."[13]

The commission often seemed more interested in protecting competitors from vigorous competition than in encouraging truthful advertising as a means of enhancing consumer welfare. As Pitofsky wrote in describing this period, the FTC

> acted as a surrogate enforcement arm for competitors . . . many enforcement actions against advertisers grew directly out of competitor complaints and appear to have been primarily intended to protect sellers against competition from cheaper substitutes.[14]

The FTC Changes of the 1970s

Throughout the 1970s, the commission's recognition of the importance of advertising as a source of information grew. The commission criticized restrictions on comparative advertising imposed by two television networks, for example. After informal meetings and correspondence with the FTC staff, the two networks agreed in 1972 to permit advertising that named competitors. In 1979 the commission

---

[13]American Bar Association, *Report of the ABA Commission to Study the Federal Trade Commission* (1969), p. 39 (1969 ABA Report).

[14]Pitofsky, "Beyond Nader," p. 674.

11

adopted a policy statement in support of comparative advertising and in opposition to restrictions imposed by broadcasters or self-regulatory bodies. Moreover, it stated that standards for substantiation should be no different for comparative advertising and unilateral claims. [15]

Closely paralleling the commission's growing recognition of the significance of advertising for competition, the Supreme Court has extended First Amendment protection to commercial speech. In the landmark decision of *Virginia State Board of Pharmacy*, the Court overturned a state ban on price advertising for prescription drugs. [16] The Court focused on the "strong interest in the free flow of commercial information" because a market economy depends on informed consumer decisions to achieve efficient resource allocation. [17] The Court has continued to recognize the value of advertising in cases involving both complete prohibitions on advertising and less sweeping restrictions on particular advertising techniques. As the Court noted in 1988,

> The free flow of commercial information is valuable enough
> to justify imposing on would-be regulators the costs of
> distinguishing the truthful from the false, the helpful from
> the misleading, and the harmless from the harmful. [18]

This study will show that some of the current efforts to restrain health and environmental advertising are constitutionally dubious. The FTC itself has strongly supported efforts to strike down restrictions on truthful commercial speech on First Amendment grounds. In 1989, for example, it filed an amicus curiae brief before the Supreme Court, arguing that

> the State's absolute prohibition of truthful certification and
> specialization claims by attorneys violates the First
> Amendment. Such communications, like other forms of
> protected commercial speech, facilitate the proper func-

---

[15]16 CFR 14.15.

[16]Virginia State Board of Pharmacy v. Virginia Citizens Consumer Council, Inc., 425 U.S. 748 (1976).

[17]Ibid., p. 764.

[18]Shapero v. Kentucky Bar Association, 108 S. Ct. 1916, 1924 (1988), quoting Zauderer v. Office of Disciplinary Counsel, 471 U.S. 626, 646 (1985).

tioning of a market economy by providing consumers with information about the nature and quality of services available from competing practitioners.[19]

As the commission noted, the Court's decisions involving commercial speech "recognize the important function that commercial speech serves in a market economy."[20]

During the 1970s the commission began to remove restrictions on advertising. Using consumer protection theories, the commission initiated a rulemaking to remove state restrictions on advertising prices of prescription drugs in 1975. The next year it initiated the Trade Regulation Rule on Advertising of Ophthalmic Goods and Services, which was promulgated in 1978.[21] Using antitrust theories, the commission also challenged private restraints on advertising contained in professional codes of ethics.[22] Each of these actions was predicated on the belief that advertising provides information to consumers that is essential to a well-functioning competitive marketplace.

Past and present FTC officials have long been unanimous in their belief that truthful advertising is an important competitive weapon that should be encouraged. Robert Pitofsky, observing the changes that occurred in FTC enforcement during the 1970s, wrote that "the major recent programs designed . . . [to regulate advertising] are based on a revised and more sensible view of the function of advertising in the market and should result in higher levels of consumer welfare."[23] And former chairman and commissioner Michael Pertschuk wrote, "Overregulation of advertising can chill aggressive competition and impose fruitless burdens on a shaky economy."[24]

---

[19]*Brief for the Federal Trade Commission as Amicus Curiae, at 8, Peel v. Attorney Registration and Disciplinary Commission*, no. 88-1775 (1989).

[20]Ibid., p. 17.

[21]*Federal Register*, vol. 43 (1978), pp. 23, 992, suspended in part and remanded, American Optometric Association v. FTC, 626 F.2d 896 (D.C. Cir. 1980). The Prescription Drug rulemaking was ultimately terminated as moot in light of the Supreme Court's decision in Virginia Board of Pharmacy.

[22]*American Medical Association*, 94 FTC 701 (1979); *American Dental Association*, 94 FTC 403 (1979).

[23]Pitofsky, "Beyond Nader," p. 701.

[24]*FTC Review (1977–1984), A Report Prepared by a Member of the Federal Trade*

State Enforcement of Abandoned FTC Views

Unfortunately, some state enforcement authorities have not yet accepted the new wisdom. Instead these states, particularly during the 1980s, pursued the symptoms of vigorous competition, much as the commission did until the 1970s. The likely consequence is the suppression of information important for consumer choices.

Perhaps the clearest example of the states' failure to appreciate the importance of advertising as a means of informing consumers is the June 1988 resolution of the National Association of Attorneys General (NAAG) on health claims, calling on the federal Food and Drug Administration to restore its prohibition on all claims about the relationship between diet and disease on food labels.[25] As the FTC staff recognized in commenting on the FDA's proposals,

> Truthful health information in both food labeling and advertising offers a powerful means of providing consumers with information that may enable them to improve their health. Manufacturers may respond to the greater opportunity to use truthful health claims in marketing their products by devoting additional resources to producing information about diet and health. Moreover, allowing food manufacturers greater latitude to emphasize the health benefits of their products is likely to increase demand for products with those benefits and thus increase incentives to produce such products. The FDA's action in removing its prior ban on such information on food labels can thus lead to a healthier population.[26]

Commission Together with Comments from Other Members of the Commission for the Subcommittee on Oversight and Investigations of the House Committee on Energy and Commerce, 98th Congress, 2d Session, 1984, p. 242. Of course, these statements are sufficiently general to be hard to challenge. Nevertheless, since 1970, as this chapter and the next two document, the commission has retreated from the harsh skepticism of the benefits of advertising it once held. Individual commission actions may still be questionable, either as being too permissive or too restrictive, but, we argue, the general trend is clear.

[25]"National Association of Attorneys General Resolution on Health Claims in Food Labeling," reprinted in *NAAG Consumer Protection Reports*, (June/July 1988), p. 3. On January 2, 1990, attorneys general of thirty-four states filed comments to the FDA, again recommending a prohibition on health claims.

[26]*Comments of the Bureaus of Competition, Consumer Protection, and Economics of*

The commission itself has long recognized the importance of encouraging, rather than prohibiting, health information in advertising. When advertising claims began linking cholesterol and heart disease in the 1960s, the commission brought several cases to ensure that the advertising accurately represented the evidence. It did not, however, seek to prohibit the claims; indeed, it expressly rejected a staff recommendation to do so when it proposed the Food Advertising Rule in 1974.[27] The growing evidence of the benefits of a low-fat, low-cholesterol diet, as well as the significant dietary changes that have occurred, amply attest to the wisdom of the commission's policy of permitting such claims.[28]

---

the Federal Trade Commission, on Health Messages on Food Labels and Labeling (1988, p. 10). The commission approved these comments, with two commissioners dissenting. The dissenters indicated that they did not disagree with the staff's conclusion. On January 5, 1990, the commission staff again filed comments to the FDA, taking the position it had previously. The commission approved these comments, with one commissioner dissenting. As chapter 5 discusses, Congress has now legislated in the health claims area.

[27]See Federal Register, vol. 39 (1974), pp. 39,842 and 39,850. The commission did, however, solicit comment on the staff proposal. When the staff report was issued at the close of the rulemaking record in 1978, the staff's recommended rule would have permitted such claims but required a disclosure that there was controversy. This recommendation, which the commission rejected in 1981, seems anachronistic at best.

[28]Information about cholesterol, for example, is associated with a significant decline in egg consumption. Brown and Schrader estimate that per capita egg consumption was reduced 16 to 25 percent by 1987, estimated over the period 1955–1987 or 1966–1987. See Deborah J. Brown and Lee F. Schrader, "Cholesterol Information and Shell Egg Consumption," American Journal of Agricultural Economics, vol. 72 (1990), p. 548. Consumption of fat also appears to have declined. Popkin et al. report consumption patterns among U.S. women in 1977 and 1985. Their data indicate significant declines in consumption of foods they identify as high fat. Because the article reports consumption of foods in grams per capita, discerning precise changes in fat consumption is difficult. Total consumption of "high fat" foods declined 18 percent. Total food consumption declined less than 2 percent. Using the midpoint of the estimated grams of fat per 100 grams of each food group reported in the article, with 25 grams assumed for foods with more than 20 grams of fat, total fat consumption from these high-fat foods declined 18 percent, or 7.5 grams per capita. Using 35 grams of fat for the open-ended category, the decline was still over 7 grams, approximately 11 percent. Calculated from Barry M. Popkin, Pamela S. Haines, and Kathleen C. Reidy, "Food Consumption Trends of U.S. Women: Patterns and Determinants between 1977 and 1985," American Journal of

A study by the FTC's Bureau of Economics demonstrates the benefits of health claims. The study examined the changes in the market for high-fiber cereals since Kellogg began advertising for All-Bran. The ad referenced the National Cancer Institute's (NCI) recommendation that diets high in fiber may reduce the risk of some kinds of cancer. The Bureau of Economics analyzed two periods. In the first, prior to 1985, only government and non-commercial sources provided information about fiber consumption and cancer. In the second period, following 1985, commercial advertising and labeling began. Scientific evidence of the link between fiber consumption and cancer developed rapidly through the 1970s and 1980s; but between 1978 and 1984, before commercial promotion, the study found no significant shift in consumption of higher-fiber cereals. Once commercial promotion began, however, a significant increase did occur.[29]

The manner in which both manufacturers and consumers responded to commercial promotion is revealing. Cereal manufacturers developed new products. Although many new fiber cereals were introduced after 1978, the study found that cereals introduced between 1979 and 1984 contained an average of 1.7 grams of fiber per ounce while those introduced between 1985 and 1987 averaged 2.6 grams of fiber per ounce. Regarding the impact on consumers, the study found significant differences in female choices of cereals across demographic groups before commercial promotion. (Consumption data were available only for women.) Women who either had less education, smoked, lived in households without a male head, or were not white chose lower-fiber cereals than other women. After commercial promotion of health claims began, with the exception of differences by education level, all the differences were reduced. In short, health claims in advertising and on labels encouraged consumption

---

Clinical Nutrition, vol. 49 (1989), p. 1,307, tables 1, 2, and 4. Studies of particular populations support the same conclusions. See Philip J. Garry et al., "Changes in Dietary Patterns over a Six-Year Period in an Elderly Population," *Annals of the New York Academy of Sciences*, vol. 561 (1989), p. 104; James L. Cresanta et al., "Trends in Fatty Acid Intakes of Ten-Year-Old Children, 1973 to 1982," *Journal of the American Dietary Association*, vol. 88 (1988), p. 178.

[29]Critics of this study claim that it does not support the FTC approach to advertising because the ads involved were precleared by government agencies. This claim is incorrect. Although the original Kellogg campaign was a cooperative effort with the NCI, the numerous other health claims ads during the period the study analyzed were not preapproved.

changes, especially among those least likely to know of the NCI's recommendation from other sources.[30]

Finally, and of great importance, the study found no evidence that consumers overreacted to health claims. There was no tendency for individuals to consume unusually large amounts of fiber cereals, nor did any of the groups that increased their fiber consumption following health claims achieve the level of consumption of the most educated consumers.[31]

As we will discuss in detail in subsequent chapters, a group of states pursued health claims for foods made by various national advertisers. At least some of the states were apparently seeking to implement the NAAG resolution in these investigations. One assistant attorney general involved in these investigations stated, "Heart attacks are way too serious to put on cereal boxes or in 30-second TV spots."[32]

This failure to understand the importance of health information in ads effectively sought to reverse a long-standing and highly beneficial federal advertising policy. To the contrary, heart attacks are way too serious for us to prohibit information that may help consumers to reduce the risk. More nutrition information in food advertising would increase the incentives for product improvement; prohibiting such information reduces the likelihood of beneficial change. The parallel to the FTC's long-abandoned policy restricting tar and nicotine claims for cigarettes could hardly be clearer.[33]

The manner in which some states are pursuing price advertising will also produce anticompetitive effects and suppress useful information, a concern noted also by the 1989 Report of the American Bar Association Section on Antitrust Law's special committee to study the role of the Federal Trade Commission.[34] The initial effect

---

[30]BE Fiber Study, pp. 3, 87.

[31]Moreover, consumers did not overreact by eating cereal with greater amounts of sodium and fat. The preexisting trend toward lower sodium and fat consumption continued. Ibid., p. 41.

[32]Richard Gibson, "Kellogg Tries to Blunt the Attacks on Cereal Makers' Health Claims," *Wall Street Journal*, August 31, 1989.

[33]Moreover, the assumption that all (or most) health claims harm consumers is suspect under the Supreme Court decisions discussed earlier in this chapter. In chapter 5, we illustrate this point in discussing the FDA's proposed rules under the new federal labeling statute.

[34]1989 ABA Report, pp. 36–37.

of the extensive disclosure requirements in NAAG's 1987 guidelines on airline price advertising was apparently to discourage such advertising.[35] The states' 1989 guidelines on rental car advertising raise similar risks. Some states have attacked invoice price advertising by automobile dealers (for instance, "2 percent over Factory Invoice"). But *Consumer Reports* maintains that consumers can save hundreds of dollars on a car purchase by knowing the invoice price, and it sells computer printouts of such prices.[36]

Finally, some states are seeking to prohibit such advertising terms as "50 percent off" unless substantial sales are made at the higher price.[37] Causing consumers to pay more hardly seems worthy of the name "consumer protection." Moreover, price is surely among the most fundamental pieces of information that consumers need in a competitive marketplace. Regulatory policies should encourage, rather than discourage, price advertising.[38]

Even in states among the most active in bringing consumer protection cases that are likely to suppress information, state antitrust officials have been more inclined to recognize the competitive value

---

[35]The Managing Director of Advertising for American Airlines stated that "the industry got away from a lot of price advertising because of the guidelines . . . that probably made the industry stop fare advertising on a large scale." Jennifer Lawrence, "Airlines Win First NAAG Bout," *Advertising Age* (February 6, 1989), p. 8. A federal district court enjoined enforcement of the NAAG guidelines in 1989, finding that they were preempted by the Federal Aviation Act. That decision was upheld by the 5th Circuit, Trans World Airlines v. Mattox, U.S. App. Lexis 4712, cert. denied, 111 S.Ct. 307 (1990). In Morales v. TWA, 112 S.Ct. 2031 (1992), the Supreme Court upheld the finding that fare advertising provisions were preempted.

[36]"How to Shop Smart for a New Car," *Consumer Reports*, vol. 54 (April 1989), p. 203. An advertisement for the Auto Price Service appears at *Consumer Reports*, vol. 53 (April 1988), p. 206. A printout for a single car is $11; for two cars, $20, and for each additional car, $7.

[37]See, for example, "J.C. Penney Agrees to Document Sales of Jewelry as Deception Suit Continues," *Antitrust and Trade Regulation Report*, vol. 58 (January 4, 1990), p. 16.

[38]In part, state activity against price advertising may reflect the fact that, although the FTC policy toward allegedly deceptive pricing changed in the 1970s, the commission never revised its 1964 Guides against Deceptive Pricing, 16 CFR 233. See 1989 ABA Report, p. 43. The "substantial sales" standard that states are seeking to enforce, however, is one that dates from the commission's 1958 guides, "Guides against Deceptive Pricing," *Federal Register*, vol. 23 (October 15, 1958), p. 7,965, and is expressly disavowed in the 1964 Guides. 16 CFR 233.1(b).

of advertising. Texas's suit under state antitrust laws against the major manufacturers of infant formula also included as a defendant the American Academy of Pediatrics, which has long opposed advertising of infant formulas directly to parents. The suit alleges that the effects of that policy, and efforts to enforce it in cooperation with other manufacturers "were to prevent Carnation from using direct advertising to inject new competition into the infant formula market [and] to deprive parents of potentially valuable and truthful information about infant formula."[39]

Advertising and the Law—Conclusion

That advertising is an important aid to effective competition has been unanimously accepted among FTC commissioners at least since the mid-1970s. When advertising is permitted to convey information effectively, it can spur better products and competitive prices. Some state actions, however, reflect a hostility toward advertising held by the commission in the 1960s but long since abandoned.

The hostility toward advertising revealed in these state positions reflects a fundamental distrust of market outcomes. We defer until chapter 8 a discussion of the reasons why the states and the FTC take different approaches to advertising. In any event, under the modern FTC view the market, regulated to prevent deception, accurately reflects consumer desires. In this view, consumers should make the ultimate decisions regarding the appropriate diet and the appropriate environmental attributes of products for themselves. Under the view of some states, mirroring an earlier FTC, a government agency must identify the appropriate diet or the appropriate environmental attributes of a product and then control the available information to channel consumers in the desired direction. It is thus no accident that, as we will see in the next several chapters, those who hold the latter view will apply principles that allow advertising routinely to be found deceptive, even if it misleads only "fools" or merely fails to provide complete information.

---

[39]*Texas v. Abbot Laboratories, American Academy of Pediatrics, Bristol-Myers Squibb Co., Mead Johnson and Co., and Ross Laboratories,* Case no. 91-13079, Travis County, Texas, 331 Judicial District, Complaint, p. 15 (filed September 17, 1991).

3

The Interpretation Problem

COMMUNICATION WITH CONSUMERS is difficult. Attracting and holding the consumer's attention long enough to convey a message challenges any advertiser's ingenuity. In advertising, with its inevitable pressures to summarize and compress the message, one cannot prevent some consumer somewhere from misinterpreting the communication. Of course, such misunderstanding is not confined to advertising. Academic studies of other brief communications, such as excerpts from news broadcasts or magazine articles, indicate that miscomprehension of the intended message is relatively common, usually for one-quarter to one-third of the audience.[1]

Whether intentional or not, an advertisement that affirmatively misleads ordinary consumers about a product impairs the efficient operation of competitive markets and should be stopped.[2] Most advertising, however, conveys truthful and useful information to the overwhelming majority of consumers who see it. If that advertising is

---

[1]*Broadcast*: Jacob Jacoby, Wayne D. Hoyer, and D. A. Sheluga, *Miscomprehension of Televised Communications* (November 1980). See also *Journal of Marketing*, vol. 46 (1982), p. 12 for a summary of the study, critical comments on its validity, and a rejoinder. *Print*: Jacob Jacoby and Wayne D. Hoyer, "The Comprehension/Miscomprehension of Print Communication: Selected Findings," *Journal of Consumer Research*, vol. 15 (1989), p. 434.

[2]We use the phrase "affirmatively misleads ordinary consumers" to rule out cases based on that fraction of consumers who would misunderstand any message about the product in question, however truthful and complete it might be. Problems arise when the net effect of exposure to the ad is to increase the amount of misinformation in the marketplace. Moreover, our conclusion that such ads should be stopped flows from our belief that common law rules against deception benefit consumers. We support FTC regulation of advertising because, procedurally, private remedies, such as small claims court and class actions, frequently are ineffective against deceptive advertising. For a discussion of these points, see Timothy J. Muris, "Consumer Protection in the 1980s," speech before the National Association of Manufacturers, March 10, 1983.

prohibited because "wayfaring men, though fools" might misinterpret it in a misleading fashion, then information is denied to the majority. Such a policy interferes with the transmission of information in the marketplace and reduces consumer welfare. As a major study of the FTC concluded:

> If any of the aforementioned kinds of information [name, price, terms of sale, possible substitutes, performance, durability] are to be protected, some credulous buyers will be deceived. About that fact there can be no doubt. Still, a balance between their plight and the needs of their less gullible counterparts must be found. Some sorts of messages must be either complex or noninformative. If complexity confuses, perhaps some confusion is acceptable.[3]

The FTC's Approach to the Interpretation Problem

By the 1940s, the commission's ability to prohibit ads that might mislead even the gullible was well established. Through the 1960s the commission often took its authority under this so-called "fools test" quite literally.[4] It challenged claims for a permanent hair dye on the theory that consumers might believe that the product would color hair that had not yet grown out.[5] It found that the name "New Bedford" rug implied domestic manufacture, even though the label disclosed the product's foreign origin on the same label in virtually the same size type.[6] In another case

> the Commission objected to respondent's assertion that his book contained "Everything you've ever wanted to know—

---

[3]George J. Alexander, *Honesty and Competition: False Advertising Law and Policy under FTC Administration* (1967), p. 227.

[4]The fools test is based on an early court opinion declaring that the commission:

> should have the discretion, undisturbed by the courts, to insist if it chooses "upon a form of advertising clear enough so that, in the words of the prophet Isaiah, 'wayfaring men, though fools, shall not err therein.' "

Charles of the Ritz Distributors Corp. v. FTC, 143 F.2d 676,680 (2d Cir. 1944), quoting General Motors Corp. v. FTC, 114 F.2d 33, 36 (2d Cir. 1940), cert. denied, 312 U.S. 682 (1941).

[5]Clairol, Inc., 33 FTC 1450 (1941).

[6]Stephen Rug Mills, 34 FTC 958 (1942).

on every conceivable subject." It solemnly found that the book did not contain everything everyone has ever wanted to know on every conceivable subject.[7]

As recently as 1962, the commission challenged the claim that yogurt was "nature's perfect food that science made better," because a person could not subsist on a diet of yogurt alone.[8] The commission's literalistic pursuit of perfection in the case of measurements of rug sizes as well described by Alexander:

> Is a rug appropriately designated 9 feet by 12 feet if it measures 104 inches by 139 inches? If one rounds off the inches, yes. For false-representation purposes, no, though 106 inches by 142 inches might qualify. Is the size correctly described if the word *approximately* precedes the size in feet? No. Suppose one gives both the approximate size in feet and the correct number of inches as well, calling the first *approximate* and the second *actual*? Still deceptive.[9]

The costs of such a policy are apparent. In the case of rug sizes, for example, what most consumers need to know is that the rug is approximately nine feet by twelve feet; precise dimensions seldom matter. Rounding rules are a reasonable way to provide this information. Those consumers who want precision presumably know they do and can act accordingly. The commission's policy in the 1960s, however, made it highly difficult for manufacturers to provide information; consumers had to do the calculations for themselves.[10]

The commission's retreat from the "fools test" began in 1963. In the Kirchner case, the commission permitted claims that a swimming aid designed to be worn under a bathing suit was "thin

---

[7]Alexander, *Honesty and Competition*, pp. 99–100, discussing National Committee for Education, 39 FTC 171 (1944).

[8]Dannon Milk Prods., Inc., 61 FTC 840 (1962).

[9]Alexander, *Honesty and Competition*, p. 47. The cases are Gimbel Bros., 61 FTC 1051 (1962), and Providence Import Co., 58 FTC 89 (1961).

[10]For those businesses that wish to communicate to consumers interested in the dimensions measured by feet, disclosing the measurements in inches will not do. It will be a rare consumer who can convert inches to feet easily in his or her head; for the others, there seems no reason to require that they perform the calculations when they did not desire the precision such calculations imply.

and invisible" when it was literally neither, noting:

> A representation does not become "false and deceptive"
> merely because it will be unreasonably misunderstood by
> an insignificant and unrepresentative segment of the class
> of persons to whom the representation is addressed.[11]

That same year, the commission dismissed charges that a charcoal
briquette advertised for its "hickory-kissed flavor" had represented
that the product was made from wood,[12] and the next year it dismissed
charges that a television tube was represented as "new" even though
the package and the tube itself disclosed that it was made from
recycled glass.[13]

Throughout the 1970s, the commission continued to shift its
focus to protect ordinary viewers of advertisements, rather than the
most credulous. In *National Dynamics*, the commission asked
"whether the interpretation is reasonable in light of the claims made
in the advertisement."[14] Debate about the meaning of advertising in
the Listerine case focused on the impression the advertising conveyed
to the "average listener";[15] in a case involving encyclopedia sales,
the commission stated that "the important criterion is the net impression that it [the sales presentation] is likely to make on the general
populace."[16]

To ensure uniform consideration of the significance of possible
misinterpretation of ads, in 1975 the commission adopted a Deceptive and Unsubstantiated Claims Policy Protocol as a guide for its
staff in selecting appropriate cases. The protocol asked FTC staff to
identify all messages that appear in the advertisement and to estimate
the proportion of consumers that receive each such message. Along
with a number of questions designed to assess the likely consumer
injury from the claims, the protocol sought to focus case selection on

---

[11]Heinz W. Kirchner, 63 FTC 1282, 1290 (1963).

[12]Quaker Oats Co., 63 FTC 2017 (1963).

[13]Westinghouse Electric Corp., 64 FTC 884 (1964). We doubt that this historical
use of the term "recycled" would meet the standards the states have proposed for
current environmental advertising. See chapter 6.

[14]National Dynamics Corp., 82 FTC 488, 524 (1973).

[15]Warner-Lambert Co., 86 FTC 1398, 1415, n. 4 (1975).

[16]Grolier, Inc., 91 FTC 315, 430 (1978).

claims that mattered most to a substantial proportion of the audience.

Perhaps the commission's shift in emphasis during the 1970s is most clearly indicated in some of the cases that it initiated but later dismissed. In 1971, for example, the commission challenged nutritional advertising for Wonder Bread. Among other allegations, the complaint contended that claims stating that Wonder Bread was fortified with nutrients implied that the product was a unique source of nutrients, distinct from other enriched breads, and that Wonder Bread would supply "all nutrients" essential to healthy growth. The Administrative Law Judge (ALJ) found that "only a small and insignificant percentage" of consumers would so interpret the ads, and he dismissed the charges. The commission agreed.[17]

Similarly, in 1974 the commission issued a complaint against the California Milk Producers Advisory Board, challenging the slogan "every body needs milk" because it allegedly implied that milk is essential for all individuals, even those who are allergic to it. In 1979 the ALJ dismissed the complaint, stating that "it would be unreasonable to judge respondent's advertising to be 'unfair, false, misleading and deceptive' because of this less than 1 percent segment of the population [who might be allergic to milk]."[18] The staff did not appeal.

By the 1980s, there was a consensus at the commission that the fools test was dead. Although the commission continued to consider any particular vulnerabilities of the audience to which an advertisement was directed, it no longer sought to protect the ignorant, the unthinking, and the credulous from every possible misinterpretation. As Commissioner Pertschuk testified before the Senate Subcommittee for Consumers, "The law in 1963 . . . essentially discard[ed] the idea that the commission can really defend the foolish."[19]

The decline of the fools test reflected growing acceptance of the economic importance of advertising, as discussed in chapter 2.

---

[17]ITT Continental Baking Co., 83 FTC 865 (1973). On another issue in that case, the commission reversed the administrative law judge (ALJ) and held that the ads did imply that Wonder Bread was "an extraordinary food for producing dramatic growth in children."

[18]California Milk Producers Advisory Board, 94 FTC 429, 547 (1979).

[19]U.S. Congress, Senate, Senate Committee on Commerce, Science and Transportation, *Hearings Before the Subcommittee on Consumers*, 98th Congress, 1st Session (1983), p. 65.

Straining to find interpretations to protect the gullible would greatly reduce the benefits of advertising, benefits that by the early 1980s were widely accepted within the commission and in the academic world. Moreover, the commission had been subjected to withering criticism and ridicule for using the fools test, some of which we have cited in this chapter. The 1969 ABA report was a source of such criticism, and those at the commission in the 1970s seemed determined to avoid the ridicule that the fools test caused.

When in 1983 the commission sought to synthesize its view of deception in a single policy statement,[20] however, controversy erupted. The statement, adopted by a 3–2 vote, was subsequently incorporated in litigated opinions and approved by the courts of appeals.[21] The commission majority concluded that an act or practice was deceptive if it was a material representation that was "likely to mislead the consumer acting reasonably in the circumstances." The minority believed that an act or practice was deceptive if it had the "tendency or capacity to mislead" a substantial number of consumers in a material respect.

Given the controversy that surround the Deception Policy statement, it is easy to lose sight of one simple fact: all of the commissioners agreed that the fools test is bad law and bad policy. The policy statement seeks to protect the interest of ordinary consumers in the free flow of information by stating that only reasonable interpretations of advertising claims are actionable. The dissenting commissioners agreed, writing that "under the traditional standard or the most recent version of the new standard the consumer—and the commission—must interpret an advertisement reasonably."[22] The minority seeks to achieve the same objective by requiring that a "substantial number," generally 20–25 percent, share the misleading interpretation.[23] Despite the difference in language, the objective is the same.

---

[20]"FTC Policy Statement on Deception," reprinted in *Antitrust and Trade Regulation Report*, vol. 4, (par. 13, 205 CCH 1983).

[21]Cliffdale Assocs. Inc., 103 FTC 110 (1984); Southwest Sunsites, Inc., 105 FTC 7 (1985), aff'd, 785 F.2d 1431 (9th Cir.), cert. denied, 479 U.S. 828 (1986); Thompson Medical Co., 104 FTC 648 (1984), aff'd, 791 F.2d 189 (D.C. Cir. 1986), cert. denied, 479 U.S. 1086 (1987).

[22]Patricia P. Bailey and Michael Pertschuk, "The Law of Deception: The Past as Prologue," *American University Law Review*, vol. 33 (1984), pp. 849, 858, n. 49.

[23]Ibid., pp. 883, 890–91.

As Commissioners Patricia Bailey and Pertschuk wrote:

> The law presumes, absent contrary evidence, that in making product claims or promises to perform, sellers have used words in their "ordinary and commonly accepted understanding." That is not to say that the commission can hold a company to the literal meaning of its words when such an interpretation is bizarre or idiosyncratic, although early court interpretations suggested that it could. The commission has recognized that it cannot hold a seller liable for every possible interpretation of a claim or protect every member of the purchasing public. Furthermore, "Neither the courts nor the Commission should freely speculate that the viewing public will place a patently absurd interpretation on an advertisement." What the commission must determine is whether a significant number of the consumers to whom a representation is directed could be misled.[24]

The real controversy was not about reasonable interpretations (or about materiality, as we discuss below); rather, it was over the commission's expertise and discretion to interpret claims. Despite agreement that the commission did not and should not protect the gullible, the minority was reluctant to disavow the commission's authority to do so.[25] The majority believed that the commission should state its standards, and indeed some commissioners recommended that they be codified in a statutory definition. Moreover, the majority believed the commission should increase its emphasis on survey evidence of how ordinary consumers actually interpret advertising; the minority preferred to continue to rely on the commission's

---

[24]Commissioners Patricia P. Bailey and Michael Pertschuk, "Analysis of the Law of Deception," in *Deception: FTC Oversight*, U.S. Congress, House Subcommittee on Oversight and Investigations of the Committee on Energy and Commerce, 98th Congress, 2d. session (1984) pp. 146–47 (footnotes omitted).

[25]Indeed, in the Law Review version of their analysis, the second sentence of the statement quoted above was revised to read, "The Commission does not, however, hold a company to the literal meaning of its words when such an interpretation is bizarre or idiosyncratic," with a footnote stating that "early court decisions suggest, however, that the Commission does have power under Section 5 to hold companies to literal interpretations of their advertisements." Bailey and Pertschuk, "Past as Prologue," p. 886 and n. 167.

expertise. As the dissenters later wrote about the policy statement, "This explanation [that acting reasonably in the circumstances applies to interpretations] appears to ignore the commission's traditional expertise to determine whether advertising practices are deceptive."[26] Although they recognized that extrinsic evidence is often helpful and must be considered when introduced, they were more reluctant to tie the commission's hands with an increased emphasis on evidence.

Despite this theoretical difference, in practice the commission has increasingly used and considered survey evidence since the early 1970s. Indeed, numerous litigated cases since Wonder Bread in 1971 have considered consumer surveys on the meaning of the advertising. The commission has varied in how much weight it has given to survey evidence in different cases, but rarely has it declined to consider surveys altogether, despite its presumed expertise. Against this backdrop, it is all the more troubling that some states, which are not at all expert in the interpretation of advertising, have refused to consider survey evidence.[27] Nor have they normally attempted to conduct or introduce survey evidence to support their interpretation of ads.

Similarly, there has been no real controversy at the commission concerning materiality. All have agreed that "an act or practice is deceptive only if it is misleading in a material respect,"[28] and that a representation is material if it "is likely to affect a consumer's choice of or conduct regarding a product. In other words, information that is important to consumers is material."[29] Indeed, in 1982 the commission unanimously rejected a signed consent agreement challenging, among other things, an implied claim that a company had been in business for ninety years when in fact it had only been in business for seventy years, because such a difference is unlikely to matter to consumers. Despite this well-established and universally accepted federal principle, however, some states have argued that materiality is irrelevant.[30]

---

[26]Ibid., pp. 858–59.

[27]Refusal to consider survey evidence has been reported by counsel to companies that are the subjects of state investigations.

[28]Bailey and Pertschuk, "Past as Prologue," p. 892.

[29]Ibid., p. 859 (quoting "Policy Statement on Deception," p. 20,916).

[30]The next section discusses examples of recent state cases.

Current State Activity in Interpretation

Despite the long-standing and essentially unanimous rejection of the fools test at the commission, some state officials have told companies under investigation that they apply that test.[31] Indeed, some recent state actions appear to apply the concept uncritically. The state of Wisconsin, for example, sought to seize a Lever Brothers butter substitute named "I Can't Believe It's Not Butter," apparently believing that consumers would mistake the product for butter. Lever went to federal court to protect its ability to market the product. In a consent order, the state agreed that the product name does not violate any state law, but the case illustrates the inappropriate application of long-since abandoned concepts of deception.[32]

Kraft's 1986 agreement with Texas to abandon specific advertisements claiming that Cheez Whiz was "real cheese made easy" raises similar issues. The ads disclosed that the product was "a blend of . . . Cheddar and Colby cheeses and other wholesome ingredients," but Texas alleged that the ads implied that the product was made of "all natural cheese without any other ingredients."[33] Apparently, Texas consumers either stop reading after "cheese," or they believe that "other wholesome ingredients" is a way of describing cheeses other than Cheddar and Colby. Either approach seems a bizarre or idiosyncratic interpretation that the commission decided in 1963 is not appropriate. Indeed, the case is reminiscent of one of the commission's rare losses on appeal, in which the court wrote:

> How a person with any intelligence could look at the label
> or brand upon a cake of soap or the wrapper thereof,
> containing the two descriptive words "palm and olive" oil,

---

[31]Moreover, at the states' Forum on Environmental Advertising in San Diego, in December 1990, one state official represented that several states view an advertisement as misleading if it has the capacity or tendency to mislead gullible consumers.

[32]Lever Bros. v. Richards, Calif. 89-0067-S (W.D. Wisc. filed June 22, 1989). Lever Bros. agreed to reduce the size of the word "spread" to the same size type used for "75 percent vegetable oil" and to change the phrase "flavored with sweet cream buttermilk" to "made with sweet cream buttermilk."

[33]Kraft, Inc., consent agreement, Texas Attorney General (February 14, 1986).

and be misled into believing that such words meant 100 per cent olive oil, is so incredible as to be unbelievable.[34]

Another example of state action based on extremely unlikely interpretations of advertising is a multistate challenge settled with Campbell Soup Company. Some of the ads the states challenged featured particular soups that are high in fiber, but they also mentioned other soups with different nutritional advantages. The states took the position that the high-fiber claim in the headline of the ad implied that every product mentioned in the ad was also high in fiber.[35] Although the FTC challenged a multiproduct Campbell's advertisement, this "problem" does not appear in the commission's complaint.[36]

Actions based on extreme interpretations of advertising have not been confined to food products. New York, for example, challenged advertising for adult disposable briefs, alleging that the manufacturer led consumers to believe there were no treatments for bladder control problems and that adult disposable briefs were the only way to lead a normal life.[37] The companies agreed to advise consumers to see their doctors for advice on controlling incontinence.

The NAAG's airline advertising guides also reflect a preoccupation with trivial variations in wording that make no appreciable difference to consumers. "Seats limited" is not acceptable; instead ads must say "this fare may not be available on all flights." "Restrictions apply" is apparently thought deceptive; instead advertising must say that "other significant restrictions apply." Taxes and surcharges cannot be disclosed separately; they must be added to the advertised fare. Ads cannot use the one-way fare even if the require-

---

[34]Allen B. Wrisley Co. v. FTC, 113 F.2d. 437, 440 (7th Cir. 1940).

[35]Attorneys General of California, Illinois, Iowa, Massachusetts, Minnesota, Missouri, New York, Texas, and Wisconsin, In the Matter of Campbell Soup Company, Assurance of Discontinuance (May 8, 1989).

[36]Campbell Soup Co., D. 9223 (January 25, 1989).

[37]"For the Record," *Advertising Age* (December 10, 1990), p. 55. The Procter and Gamble advertising said, for example, "I doubted I would ever work again. I have a bladder control problem. I found the protection I need with Attends." Natalie Angier, "Makers of Adult Diapers Agree to Alter Ads," *New York Times* (December 8, 1990), p. 10.

ment to purchase a round-trip ticket is disclosed; they must use the round-trip fare. The commission has not pursued such distinctions since its struggle with approximate measurements of rug sizes.

Interpretation—Conclusion

Any advertisement can cause a few to misinterpret it. Regulatory efforts to protect the foolish can deprive ordinary consumers of truthful and useful information. The commission's policies have evolved to avoid this problem, limiting challenges to interpretations that are widely shared. Too often, state actions have reduced consumer welfare because they neglected this important principle.

4

The Problem of Too Much Information

ALTHOUGH ADVERTISING is a valuable source of information for consumers, it is necessarily incomplete. Because any topic that is even moderately complicated is undoubtedly the subject of at least several books, even multipage print advertisements cannot include everything. The physical limitations of broadcast advertising are much more severe. Most such advertising is thirty seconds in length or less; the script for a typical thirty-second television advertisement includes only about sixty words.

Of course, incomplete information can be misleading. Disclosure requirements are appropriate when half-truths or significant omissions lead consumers to erroneous conclusions. Nevertheless, even incomplete information is often extremely valuable, especially when the alternative is complete ignorance. Knowing an automobile's gas mileage even without knowing its horsepower or engine size is useful. Knowing that Wonder Bread is enriched with various nutrients is valuable, even without knowing that other brands are also enriched. Knowing that a particular item can be purchased today for less than the regular price at a particular retail outlet is valuable, even without knowing that such sales are frequent.

One example of the value of even incomplete information stems from the advertising of "no cholesterol" during the 1960s and 1970s. Some advertising discussed the relationship between cholesterol and heart disease explicitly, but most simply claimed that a product had no cholesterol. Cholesterol advertising contributed to the increasing public awareness of the relationship between diet and heart disease. [1]

---

[1] In 1982, 26 percent of consumers were aware of dietary cholesterol as a risk factor in heart disease, a figure that increased to 40 percent in 1986. Dale Blumenthal,

Indeed, the marketing director of a pharmaceutical company stated that advertising by fats-and-oils manufacturers was probably the single most important factor in consumer understanding of the significance of saturated fats.[2] Moreover, diets have changed substantially, reducing the risk of heart attack.[3] Even though it was incomplete, advertising of cholesterol in the 1960s and 1970s was therefore valuable, contributing to reductions in the risk of heart disease.

Excessive disclosure requirements cause problems for consumers. Advertisements are brief in part because of cost, but a more fundamental reason operates as well: consumer attention is a scarce resource. Consumers are exposed to hundreds of advertisements each day; they do not and cannot pay careful attention to each one. Disseminating an advertisement does not ensure that it will be noticed. Even when noticed, commercial messages are not necessarily retained; even when a message is remembered, consumers may not recall the name of the brand that sponsored the message. Effective communication requires a message that is noticeable, short, and to the point.

Numerous studies have shown that providing too much information can actually lead to worse decisions, not better ones—a phenomenon known as "information overload."[4] The reason is straightforward: consumers must process the information before they use it. The longer and more complicated the message, the more likely that

---

"The Health-Diet Link: Charting a Rising Awareness," *FDA Consumer* (October 1989), p. 23.

[2]"Health Claim Restraint by Responsible Firms Predicted," *Food Chemical News* (March 31, 1986), p. 35.

[3]Indeed, the Centers for Disease Control cited evidence of a downward trend in serum cholesterol and increased knowledge of the relationship between diet and heart disease as evidence of substantial progress in achieving one of their 1990 national health objectives. See *Morbidity and Mortality Weekly Report*, vol. 40 (1991), p. 459.

[4]See, for example, Kevin Lane Keller and Richard Staelin, "Effects of Quality and Quantity of Information on Decision Effectiveness," *Journal of Consumer Research*, vol. 14, p. 200 (1987). Although information overload has been a controversial subject, even if consumers are given unlimited time to consider the data, there is virtually no dispute that excessive information rapidly overwhelms consumers' abilities to remember and utilize facts from advertising. The classic study on the limitations of information processing is George A. Miller, "The Magical Number Seven, Plus or Minus Two: Some Limits on Our Capacity for Information Processing," *Psychological Review*, vol. 63 (1956), p. 81.

consumers will ignore it. Even if they pay some attention to it, the likelihood of errors in understanding and remembering is greater the more detailed the message. Such errors are particularly likely with broadcast advertising, because consumers cannot look back to reexamine it. These difficulties led the FTC staff to recommend, in a 1979 policy review session, that "broadcast disclosures should be simple, serving primarily to motivate information search at the point of sale."[5]

Understanding how consumers process and use information reveals another important factor in disclosure requirements. Timing matters. A company can provide information on product labels that is extremely useful but would be nearly useless in advertising. Information on the proper dosage for over-the-counter drugs, for example, is essential on product labels, but it has little value in advertising. Moreover, labels can be a useful reference for detailed nutritional information, such as a product's vitamin content; but the same amount of information in advertising is likely to produce severe information overload.

Even if information-overload problems are avoided, advertisers may simply stop making claims that require extensive disclosures. Faced with the costs of devoting a significant portion of each ad to disclosures rather than to a selling message, advertisers have the incentive to avoid such claims entirely. Regulatory requirements that give advertisers the choice between nearly complete information or no information will often leave consumers with no information. And if advertising cannot inform consumers of product differences, companies have less incentive to improve products in ways that consumers would desire. When companies can inform consumers of product differences, competition increases the incentive to improve products. Advertisers that possess superior characteristics will note that fact in their advertisements, causing competitors to respond, either through product improvement or through pointing out their superior attributes. The result is an increase in information to consumers and an ability to make better purchasing decisions.[6]

---

[5]*Consumer Information Remedies* (June 1, 1979), p. 315. (FTC Policy Review Session).

[6]Sellers even have incentives to disclose certain negative attributes of their products. As discussed in Paul H. Rubin, "The Economics of Regulating Deception," *Cato Journal*, vol. 10 (1991), p. 667, consumers will rationally assume that advertise-

The FTC's Approach to the Information Glut

Over time, the commission has come to recognize that advertising cannot do everything. The early 1970s were the heyday of disclosure proposals at the commission, most often embodied in proposed rules. Indeed, these proposals sometimes seemed to be based on the belief that each advertisement should be an encyclopedic reference regarding the product. To improve disclosures, the commission sought to increase its consumer research sophistication, hiring academic marketing scholars to provide expertise and advice. In 1979 a staff task force of marketing experts, economists, attorneys, and others reported to the commission in a policy review session on consumer information remedies. The report included a review of the marketing literature on information-processing problems and a careful analysis of the likely impact of disclosure requirements. Although oriented toward improving the effectiveness of disclosures, the report also addressed the need to balance disclosures against the risk of discouraging information altogether. It noted:

> The tension between avoiding consumer deception while maximizing the flow of truthful speech is apparent. The Commission must decide whether the total information environment would be improved by the elimination of particular misleading claims, or whether consumers would be better off with some slightly misleading information about an attribute rather than no information at all.[7]

The commission's emerging understanding of the limitations of advertising, as well as its capabilities, is reflected in the fate of many of its early disclosure proposals. In the Wonder Bread complaint issued in 1971, for example, the commission also challenged adver-

---

ments without critical information imply that the product is at the lowest level regarding the omitted attribute. Products with quality levels above the minimum thus have incentives to advertise that fact. Consider the tar derby, discussed in chapter 2. The products that had low tar advertised that fact, leading consumers to conclude that products not mentioning tar probably had high tar. Pauline M. Ippolito and Alan D. Mathios, "The Regulation of Science-based Claims in Advertising," *Journal of Consumer Policy*, vol. 13 (1990), p. 413, report high levels of disclosure for all but the worst products in cereals, bread, butter, and margarine. Similarly, lower tar cigarettes are more likely to disclose tar content on the package.

[7]FTC, *Consumer Information Remedies*, pp. 283–84.

tising claims for Hostess Snack Cakes. When the snacks were first enriched with vitamins, ITT advertised that fact, pointing out the product's nutritional advantages over unenriched snacks. At the time, fortification of snack products represented a significant technological advance; earlier efforts had left products with an unacceptable taste. Among other charges, the complaint alleged that the advertisements were deceptive because they failed to disclose that the cakes were composed primarily of sugar.

In 1973 the commission upheld the ALJ's decision to dismiss this allegation. In rejecting the staff's argument for disclosure of sugar, the commission wrote:

> The instant case involves a nutritional claim with respect to a food product. And an absolute claim for good nutrition may well be objectionable for the reason that the advertisement omits things that should be said. On the other hand, it would be unrealistic to impose upon the advertiser the heavy burden of nutritional education, especially with respect to radio and TV commercials which in many cases are shorter than thirty seconds and seldom as long as sixty seconds. Therefore, we should not attempt to establish an overly restrictive standard of general application in this regard. To do so would be tantamount to a *de facto* ban on all nutritional advertising through the radio and TV media.[8]

The commission returned to the question of nutrition advertising when it proposed the second phase of the Food Advertising Rule in 1974. The rule would have defined "nutritious" and "nutritional parity" based on vitamin content, and it would have set specific standards for how much of a nutrient a food must contain before that nutrient could be mentioned in advertising. Any mention would have required disclosure of the percentage of the recommended daily allowance (RDA) that the product provided, and claims that a food was a unique source of nutrition or was nutritionally superior to other foods were prohibited. To say the least, the proposal would have enormously complicated any attempt to discuss nutrition in advertising. An even more ambitious third phase of the proposed rule would have required disclosures in all food advertising. The FTC did not

---

[8]ITT Continental, 83 FTC at 965.

enact these proposals. When the Pertschuk commission considered the matter in 1980, it unanimously concluded that advertising disclosures simply could not fulfill the functions of nutrition education. Advertising, the commission stated, "is not, cannot, and should not be the sole source of information on food and nutrition."[9] The ruling was put on hold and eventually terminated in 1982.

Thus, by 1980 a consensus had emerged at the commission that excessive disclosure requirements were more likely to harm consumers than to help them. That consensus held through the 1980s. Consider the commission's warranty advertising guides, adopted in 1960. The guides required that advertising that mentioned a warranty should include detailed descriptions of the warranty's limitations. Advertising had to state what product or part of the product was guaranteed, the warranty's duration, what it included and excluded, and what the consumer had to do (for example, return the product) before the manufacturer would honor the warranty. As a result, there was little advertising of warranties.[10] In 1979 the commission rejected a staff proposal to write such detailed disclosure requirements into a rule. Instead it sought comment on whether the guides should be revised or rescinded. In 1985 a unanimous commission replaced the detailed requirements with a requirement for all simple disclosure that the warranty is available for inspection (for example, "See our warranty where you shop").[11] This change reopened the possibility of warranty advertising and greater competition over warranty terms.

The Games of Chance Rule was also reconsidered in light of the new consensus about appropriate disclosure requirements. Adopted in 1969, the rule required that any advertising that mentioned the prizes in a game must disclose the exact number of prizes in each category, the odds of winning each prize (revised weekly if the game lasted longer than thirty days), the geographic area the game covered, the total number of participating retail outlets, and the termination date of the game. Particularly in broadcast advertising, these require-

---

[9]*Federal Register*, vol. 45 (1980), p. 23,705.

[10]In adopting revised guides, the commission concluded that "the disclosure requirements of the existing Guides have discouraged advertisers from promoting their warranties in advertising." *Federal Register*, vol. 53 (1985), pp. 18,462 and 18,467.

[11]Ibid.

ments imposed enormous burdens. In 1983 a unanimous commission granted a temporary exemption from the broadcast advertising disclosure provisions. Five years later, the commission issued a Notice of Proposed Rulemaking to amend the rule to replace the detailed disclosures with a notice that the information is available at participating stores.[12]

The commission's actions to eliminate excessive disclosure requirements have been uncontroversial. Commissioners with widely differing views of the appropriate role of government in the marketplace have supported them, all recognizing that extensive disclosure requirements can do more harm than good.

Current State Activity Concerning Information

Despite the federal consensus that advertising cannot do everything, some states seem to proceed from the premise that advertising must provide complete information or none at all. Consider, for example, the recent assurance-of-discontinuance agreement between Campbell Soup and nine states. The agreement ended ads claiming that diets high in fiber and low in fat may reduce the risks of some forms of cancer, and stating that bean-with-bacon soup is a good source of fiber. The states' theory is that although the soup is low in fat, it contains bacon, which is a high-fat meat, and fat is a risk factor for heart disease.[13] The theory that truthful claims about one nutrient require disclosure of other putatively undesirable ingredients, however, is precisely what the commission rejected in the ITT case—in 1973.

The failure to learn the disclosure lessons of the 1970s is also apparent in the NAAG car rental guidelines.[14] An empirical study of

---

[12]*Federal Register*, vol. 53 (1988), p. 25,503.

[13]The states did not challenge Campbell's argument that, even with bacon, the soup was still low in fat. The FTC challenged a different advertisement in the campaign that promoted a low fat, low cholesterol soup as a way to reduce the risk of heart disease without disclosing the fact that the soup is high in sodium. Because sodium is also a risk factor for heart disease, the commission's theory is a sound one if the net effect of the product as a whole is to increase the risk of heart disease. See Campbell Soup Co., D. 9223 (complaint), issued January 25, 1989. The FDA's view is closer to the states' than to the FTC's, a point we address in the next chapter. Even the FDA, however, would not require fat disclosures for a product that qualifies as low fat.

[14]"Car Rental Practices Guidelines," reprinted in *Antitrust and Trade Register Report*, vol. 56 (BNA), Special Supplement, March 16, 1989.

the guidelines tested a basic radio ad with the NAAG disclosure—
"Offer available through March 15 at participating locations, 30 cent
mileage fee per mile after first one hundred miles, collision damage
waiver 12 dollars per day, other important restrictions apply"—
against a simple alternative disclosure akin to what the commission
adopted in revising the warranty guides—"Contact an Avis reserva-
tions agent for details." Despite the differences in the costs of these
alternatives, there were essentially no differences in consumer understanding of the likelihood of restrictions in general, or of specific
restrictions, between the detailed NAAG disclosure and the simple
alternative.[15]

The empirical study also provides considerable evidence that
there is no need for a disclosure at all. In a test of the commercial
without a disclosure, 88 percent of the subjects indicated that they
felt restrictions on the offer were likely.[16] In contrast, the FTC
unanimously agreed to delete certain disclosure provisions from the
Encyclopaedia Britannica order in 1982 when the company presented
survey evidence that 80 percent of respondents understood the
message the commission wanted to convey, even without a disclosure.[17] Moreover, the modified order specified a survey protocol that
allows an advertising claim as long as 75 percent of respondents
understand that a sales representative will call.[18] Although a 75
percent comprehension level may be unacceptably low for important
health or safety information, it is entirely reasonable when the only
risk to consumers is an undesired visit from a salesman or an
unnecessary call to a car rental agent. The NAAG's apparent insis-

---

[15]John H. Murphy and Jeff I. Richards, "An Investigation of the Effects of
Disclosure Statements in Rental Car Commercials" (Department of Advertising,
University of Texas, June 1989).

[16]Ibid., pp. 13–14. Using a different measure of understanding known as the
Relative Proximity Index, which the FTC has never considered, the study found
some indication the test ad implied there were "no restrictions," but even without
disclosure there was no evidence of deception on any of the specific restrictions.
All these measures probably understate consumer understanding, however, because
the subjects were students who are probably less familiar with car rental transactions
than are the typical members of the viewing audience.

[17]Encyclopaedia Britannica, Inc., Docket no. 8908, Supplemental Submission of
Encyclopaedia Britannica, Inc. in Support of Request to Reopen Proceedings and
Set Aside or Modify Order, pp. 27–31 (October 9, 1981).

[18]Encyclopaedia Britannica, Inc., 100 FTC 500 (1982), 505–06 (modifying order).

tence on perfection in very similar circumstances stands in stark contrast.

We have already noted that the NAAG's airline guides raise similar problems of excessive disclosure requirements. The willingness to suppress information in broadcast advertising was explicit in the comment of one deputy attorney general involved in the project:

> There just may be too many limitations in broadcast for fare advertising. Broadcast may be better suited for image rather than price ads. . . . People either don't hear or don't understand that restrictions apply.[19]

As the 1989 American Bar Association report noted, "the net effect is to make price advertising more difficult."[20] And as we discussed above, the apparent outcome was to make price advertising less common.

The Information Glut—Conclusion

Excessive disclosure burdens can cause serious problems for consumers. Consumers confronted with too much information in too much detail may misinterpret the ad, or simply ignore it altogether. Advertisers faced with excessive disclosure requirements may avoid providing information. Although these principles have commanded a consensus at the FTC for well over a decade, some states have not yet accepted them. Nor, as we shall see next, has the FDA.

---

[19]Jennifer Lawrence, "Airlines Lash Out at Guidelines," *Advertising Age* (September 28, 1987), p. 28.

[20]1989 ABA Report, p. 37, n. 50.

Case Studies in Advertising Regulation

Growing state involvement in the regulation of national advertising has influenced or is likely to influence national advertising and federal regulation. Part two examines two areas of state involvement—health claims and environmental claims—in detail.

As we have seen, the FTC and the states have taken widely different approaches toward advertising regulation in general and health claims in particular. As reflected in their comments to the FDA, the states argued for banning health claims, while the FTC would allow such claims if they are supported by a "reasonable basis." With the support of food industry groups that were deeply concerned about growing state regulation of national marketing, Congress in late 1990 enacted the Nutrition Labeling and Education Act (NLEA) to regulate, among other things, health claims on food labels.[1] Chapter 5 evaluates the substantive merits of that legislation, as well as other aspects of the health claims controversy.

The dispute over environmental claims is more recent in orgin. Chapter 6 discusses the issues and contrasts the approach of the states with modern FTC advertising policy. Neither the FTC nor the Congress has spoken on the environmental-claims issue. Thus it remains to be seen whether the aggressiveness of the states will contribute to an increase in regulation, as it appears to have done in the health claims area.

---

[1] 104 Stat. 2353.

5
Health Claims

AS EXPLAINED ABOVE, truthful claims concerning the relationship between diet and disease can substantially benefit consumers.
Many people remain unaware of the mounting evidence linking diet
to various chronic diseases, and advertisements and labels can
reduce that information gap. The evidence indicates that claims
about the inverse relationship between fiber and the risk of cancer
have done precisely that, reducing the knowledge disparities among
different groups of consumers and leading to significant product
improvements.[1]

Sound regulation of health messages for foods must proceed
from a recognition that foods are not drugs *in fact*, even if certain
claims arguably make them drugs under some federal and state
regulations. The dietary modifications that have been suggested or
promoted do not appear to pose any appreciable public health risk.
The potential risks from introducing a new drug, however thoroughly
tested, are surely orders of magnitude greater. Indeed, the underlying
rationale for the statutory distinctions between the regulatory standards for foods and the more stringent controls on drugs is the
intuitive notion that the consequences of errors in deciding what to
eat are far less than the costs of erroneous decisions about drugs.

Of course, exaggerated or misleading claims about the health
benefits of particular foods or dietary modifications can harm consumers. The harm, however, is essentially economic.[2] Consumers

---

[1]See the discussion in chapter 2 of the FTC's fiber study.

[2]Noneconomic injury could occur if competing claims promoted substitute dietary
changes to achieve the same objective. A deceptive claim in such circumstances
could lead consumers to give up an effective dietary change for one that is
ineffective. Although relevant in individual cases, this possibility cannot justify
stringent general regulations, which would deprive consumers of information about
both alternatives.

might pay more for a product or might purchase one brand instead of another that tastes better. Sound regulation should prevent such injuries and therefore benefit consumers. Conversely, overly stringent regulatory requirements that inhibit or prevent truthful claims about the relationship between diet and disease create risks to public health. Fewer consumers will hear important health recommendations, and manufacturers will have greatly reduced incentives to improve products to reflect that advice. When opportunities to reduce the incidence of disease are not taken because of excessive regulatory requirements, the public's health suffers.

A trade-off between health or safety benefits and economic costs is common in consumer protection regulation. Economists and others considering such rules have long argued that even when some regulation is justified, we should not incur excessive costs in pursuit of limited benefits. This trade-off is present in considering health messages as well, but it is reversed—overregulation may produce significant public health costs in pursuit of relatively minor economic benefits.

Conceptually, several approaches to health claims are possible. A market-oriented strategy, the traditional FTC policy based on the principles discussed above, would rely on the power of truthful information to guide markets in the directions that consumers most prefer. It would preserve the benefits of current health claims and allow the possibility of similar benefits in other areas. In contrast, the states have recommended a prohibitionist approach—just say no. This approach, however, abandons entirely the important benefits that health claims can offer consumers.

A third approach, which the FDA has advocated and Congress recently adopted for food labels, is a nutrition regulation strategy. The basis for this approach is an initial decision about the kind of dietary changes that consumers "should" make. Given this conception of the "true" relationship between diet and health, the nutrition-regulation strategy seeks to control the flow of information to manipulate consumer choices. Although it relies on market mechanisms to bring about the desired product changes, the nutrition-regulation strategy is based on an essentially paternalistic judgment: if certain choices are nutritionally sound, consumers should make them.

This third approach became law late in 1990, when Congress

46

passed the Nutrition Labeling and Education Act of 1990.[3] This act, discussed in detail in section two of this chapter, overhauls federal food-labeling regulations. It mandates nutrition-labeling for most foods, including certain additional information not required on current nutrition labels. The act also establishes substantive standards to be elaborated in FDA regulations for claims on food and labeling relating nutrients to disease, and it requires prior FDA approval of the claimed relationship.[4]

In addition, the act prohibits claims that "characterize" the level of nutrients, unless the FDA has defined the characterizing term in a regulation, and in many instances it requires additional disclosures as well. By its terms, the act does not apply to food advertising, although legislation has been introduced that would extend many of the same requirements to advertising.[5] Thus the question of which strategy should be used to regulate advertising remains unresolved, and we discuss it briefly in section three of this chapter.

Business interests supported the legislation, primarily because it preempts state actions governing the same claims. Thus the statute provides for a single standard to govern all claims. The legislation, however, also provides an expanded and unique role for state enforcement: states can bring civil actions to enforce the statute in federal court, subject only to a "right of first refusal" by the FDA. The state must give notice of its intent to file and then wait thirty days. If within that time the FDA commences an informal or formal enforcement action, the state must wait an additional sixty days. At that point, the state can file, unless the FDA has settled the proceeding or is "diligently prosecuting" it in court. In addition, states are given a statutory right to intervene in any court proceedings in which the federal government is seeking to enforce the statute.[6]

The extent to which states will actually employ their option to enforce the NLEA is unclear. With some justification, the industry

---

[3]104 Stat. 2353.

[4]The provisions of the act regulating health claims are quite similar to the approach taken in the FDA's previously proposed rule to govern such claims. See *Federal Register*, vol. 55 (February 13, 1990), p. 5,176.

[5]H.R. 1662, the Nutrition Advertising Coordination Act of 1991.

[6]Nutrition Labeling and Education Act, section 4.

groups that supported the statute expect that the provision will be little used. A detailed federal regulatory scheme certainly increases the costs of state involvement. Not only must potential state enforcers master the intricacies of the regulatory regime, but they also run the risk that the FDA will take over any promising case that a state develops.

Moreover, a role that is confined to enforcement of someone else's rules is likely to reduce the political incentives for state involvement. Just as state actions under state food and drug statutes were very infrequent before NLEA, in part because of the pervasive and detailed federal regulatory structure, the state enforcement provisions of the NLEA may be seldom used. If states do seek a presence, the detailed regulatory scheme with its host of specific requirements reduces the range of policy judgments on which individual states might differ from the FDA. In addition, the FDA has taken the position in its proposed implementing rules that its interpretations of the statute and the rules are binding on state enforcers. [7]

The Statutory Standard for Health Claims

The Nutrition Labeling and Education Act distinguishes between health claims, which discuss the relationship between a nutrient and a disease or a health-related condition, and nutrient-descriptor claims, such as "no cholesterol," which "characterize" the level of a nutrient. [8]

The Act's Basic Requirements. After the next paragraph briefly summarizes the regulation of descriptor claims, we discuss health claims in detail, to illustrate the approach of the new statute.

---

[7] "If FDA advises a state that its proposed action is inconsistent with FDA's interpretation, FDA believes section 307 of the act requires that the state conform its interpretation to FDA's." *Federal Register*, vol. 56 (1991), p. 60,536. A comment submitted by thirty-two attorneys general, however, "strongly disagreed" with the FDA's view, maintaining that if there is disagreement about interpretation, "it is up to a court to decide" meaning. *State Attorneys General Comments Regarding FDA-NLEA Proposals* (February 24, 1992, p. 36).

[8] We use the terms "health messages" and "health-related claims" to encompass both health claims and nutrient descriptor claims that are health related.

Although possibly health-related, a nutrient-descriptor claim is not subject to the standards applicable to health claims.[9] Descriptor claims, however, are closely regulated. They are prohibited unless FDA has defined the particular terms used—for example, "high," "low," "reduced". In many instances they must be accompanied by extensive disclosures.[10] Moreover, the FDA's proposed implementing rules treat any content claim (such as "five grams fat per serving") as a descriptor claim, subject to regulation.[11] Indeed, the proposed definition of implied nutrient-content claims would reach many claims about ingredients: for example, "made with whole wheat" may be an implied claim of high-fiber content.[12] However truthful, content claims outside the nutrition label itself are prohibited unless the food would be permitted to claim that it is "low" in a bad nutrient or "high" in a good one. Even comparative claims must meet regulatory definitions of "more" and "less" and must be accompanied by detailed disclosures.[13]

Regarding health claims, the act establishes two basic requirements. First, claims must conform to FDA regulations. In the absence of a regulation, claims are prohibited even if true. Regulations can authorize claims only if the FDA finds "significant scientific agreement" that the claim is supported by "the totality of publicly available scientific evidence." The regulation must describe the relationship

---

[9]Food, Drug, and Cosmetics Act (FDCA), section 403 (r) (1).

[10]FDCA, section 403 (r) (2). The proposed implementing regulations reflect numerous triumphs of regulatory nitpicking over common sense. Because there are a number of chemically distinct sugars, for example, the FDA is proposing a definition of "sugars-free," but not "sugar-free." The widely understood term "sugarless" would be prohibited, because the technically correct phrase would be "sugarsless." *Federal Register*, vol. 56, p. 60,437.

[11]The FDA's proposed rules governing general nutrient content claims appear at *Federal Register*, vol. 56, p. 60,421. The specific rules applicable to descriptive terms applied to fat, fatty acids, and cholesterol appear at *Federal Register*, vol. 56 (1991), p. 60,478 (Definitions of Nutrient Content Claims).

[12]*Federal Register*, vol. 56, pp. 60,423–24.

[13]The definitions of "more" and "less" are not symmetric. To claim "less" of a nutrient, a food must have at least 25 percent less compared with the reference food. *Federal Register*, vol. 56, p. 60,451. To claim "more" of a nutrient, a food must have at least 10 percent more than the reference food. *Federal Register*, vol. 56, p. 60,453.

between the nutrient and the disease, and also the significance of the nutrient in affecting the disease. The regulation must require the claim to represent the relationship accurately and in a way that enables the public to understand the information and its significance.[14] Such a prior assessment of the evidence is of course essential to the nutrition regulation strategy. Until the FDA has conducted a detailed review of the available data, it cannot decide how it should seek to channel consumer choices.

The act's second requirement prohibits health claims for any food that contains an amount of any nutrient that increases the risk of disease to the general population. Thus, even if the rules would allow claims that, for example, calcium reduces the risk of osteoporosis, a cheese product might be prohibited from making the claim if the FDA determines that it has too much fat. The FDA can permit such claims, however, if it determines that a claim would "assist consumers in maintaining healthy dietary practices." Moreover, the label would have to disclose the condemned nutrient in immediate proximity to the claim, along with the advice to "see [side] panel for nutrition information."[15] Again, the roots of these provisions in the nutrition-regulation strategy are apparent.

As required in the statute, the FDA has issued proposed regulations addressing whether claims in ten specified areas are consistent with the act.[16] Other claims could be considered upon petition to the FDA.

---

[14]FDCA, section 403 (r) (3) (B). The regulations may not, however, require prior approval for claims that are in compliance. Nutrition Labeling and Education Act of 1990, section 3 (b) (1) (A) (vii). Thus, although the FDA must grant prior approval of the substance of health claims, it cannot require prior approval of individual labels conveying the substantive message.

[15]FDCA, section 403 (r) (3) (A) (ii).

[16]The specified areas are calcium and osteoporosis; sodium and hypertension; dietary fiber and cancer; lipids and cardiovascular disease; lipids and cancer; dietary fiber and cardiovascular disease; folic acid and neural tube defects; antioxidant vitamins and cancer; zinc and immune function in the elderly; and omega-3 fatty acids and heart disease. Nutrition Labeling and Education Act, section 3 (b) (1) (A) (vi) and (x). Other sections of the act indicate that Congress presumed that fat and saturated fat should be avoided. Significant amounts of these substances must be disclosed if a cholesterol claim is made, a requirement that is a specific example of the general principle that disclosure of significant amounts of harmful nutrients must accompany any nutrient content claim. See FDCA, section 403 (r) (2) (A) (iii), (B) (ii).

Problems with the Act. The Nutrition Labeling and Education Act's provisions regulating health claims raise several problems. First, the statute prohibits health messages in new areas until the FDA completes a rulemaking addressing the issues. This approach to health messages appears to be modeled on the process of developing monographs for over-the-counter (OTC) drugs. Unfortunately, however, the agency has been considering such monographs for more than a decade, with no resolution in sight for many categories. Health messages, where there is far less consensus about which scientific methodologies are appropriate and a far greater role for policy judgment in reaching a conclusion, may well make the OTC-monograph process look rapid. At the very least, the monograph experience hardly counsels optimism about the FDA's ability to resolve the issues quickly. The process will inevitably delay health messages substantially.

Perhaps to address concerns about possible delays, the statute sets out a relatively short timetable for dealing with petitions seeking regulations to permit additional health claims. Within one hundred days the FDA must either deny the petition or file it for further action. If the petition is filed, the agency has an additional ninety days either to deny the petition or to issue a proposed regulation to take the action requested in the petition.[17] There is no timetable, however, for issuing the final rule that may result.

Concluding the proceeding has been a substantial hurdle for OTC monographs. Of sixty-five separate drug categories for which the FDA had issued a Notice of Proposed Rulemaking (NPRM) or taken final action, final action has occurred for only twenty-nine categories. That final action was, on average, forty-six months after the NPRM.[18] Moreover, the NPRMs themselves were generally issued several years after an advance notice of proposed rulemaking that allowed for public comment on an advisory committee report that presumably took an appreciable time to prepare. If this process is even roughly indicative, health claims in areas beyond those specifically addressed in the statute will be years in coming.[19]

---

[17]FDCA, section 403 (r) (4) (A) (i).

[18]Calculated from the timetable information in the FDA's entry in the Unified Agenda of Federal Regulations, *Federal Register*, vol. 56 (April 22, 1991), p. 17,293. Categories that were consolidated with other rulemakings were excluded.

[19]For those ten areas, the FDA is required by the act to propose a rule determining

While the FDA considers its regulations, the public will wait. So, too, will the health benefits that a new message might offer. When the surgeon general or the National Cancer Institute or the National Academy of Sciences issues some new recommendation concerning diet and health, the statute prohibits any mention of that recommendation on labels until a different part of the federal government conducts a review of the scientific adequacy of the conclusion. Food manufacturers should be free to use labels to inform consumers of those conclusions, and consumers should be entitled to know about them when they are reached, not after extended further review. The FDA's administrative convenience hardly seems sufficient justification for delaying widespread knowledge of a public health recommendation that another part of the government thought was appropriate. The argument for delay is hardly stronger if the recommendation comes from an authoritative, nongovernmental source such as the American Cancer Society or the American Heart Association. The public interest in timely dissemination of such important information is far more compelling.

Although strong constitutional arguments can be mustered against most of the act based on its restrictions on truthful commercial speech, it is particularly difficult to see how the requirement for FDA rulemaking to review the conclusions of another government agency could withstand constitutional challenge.[20] The government interest involved is hardly substantial, and the restriction on truthful speech does little to advance that interest, directly or indirectly.[21]

---

whether they meet the requirements of the statute within twelve months of the date of enactment. If the rulemaking is not concluded within twenty-four months of the date of enactment, the proposed rules will be considered final. Nutrition Labeling and Education Act, section 3 (b).

[20]The nutrient description rules as proposed by FDA would for example prohibit a variety of truthful claims that are not in any sense misleading. The regulations include provisions that prohibit brand-to-brand comparisons, regulate type size to avoid "undue prominence" for truthful claims, and prohibit truthful nutrient content statements (for example, "Our product contains 10 grams of fat") unless the product meets regulatory standards. See *Comments of the Staffs of the Bureau of Economics and Consumer Protection of the FTC*, "In the Matter of Nutrition Labeling: Nutrient Content Claims, Health Claims, Ingredient Labeling, Proposed Rules," (February 25, 1992) (FTC Comment) for a number of other examples.

[21]Central Hudson Gas and Electric Corp. v. Public Services Commissioner, 447 U.S. 557 (1980).

Nor is it apparent how one might attempt to argue that the restriction is narrowly tailored to achieve its objective.[22]

A closely related problem concerns the scientific standard to apply in determining whether a particular relationship between diet and disease is adequately supported. The statute itself requires "significant scientific agreement" among qualified experts.[23] The precise meaning of the standard is unclear. The FDA's proposed rule, of which Congress was certainly aware, would have required "significant agreement." The agency indicated its tentative conclusion that a "very high" standard is necessary, but it sought comment on whether it should require a "consensus" or whether "substantial evidence" that a relationship exists should suffice.[24] Thus, as the FDA recognized in its proposed implementing rules, the statute does not require a consensus.[25] Furthermore, the FDA was "not convinced" that a "reasonable basis," which the FTC determines based on the benefits and costs of developing evidence to substantiate the claim, is enough. Thus the statute apparently will require more evidence than the benefits and costs of developing additional data would justify.

Ideally, the amount of evidence required should depend on the circumstances. The regulator should consider explicitly the consequences of erroneous decisions in determining how much evidence is enough. Two kinds of mistake are possible—consumers can mistakenly fail to rely on a true claim or they can mistakenly rely on a false claim. Each mistake has costs.

The consumer who does not learn about a true claim because of the government's action loses the benefits that the ad promises; the consumer who relies on a false claim is injured. For most claims about the relationship between diet and disease, the consequences of mistakenly approving a claim that subsequent research might disprove are relatively small and predominately economic.[26] Banning

---

[22]Board of Trustees of the State University of New York v. Fox, 492 U.S. 469 (1989).

[23]FDCA, section 403 (r) (3) (B) (i).

[24]*Federal Register*, vol. 55, p. 5,181.

[25]*Federal Register*, vol. 56 (1991), p. 60,548. The states too apparently recognize that the statute requires something less than consensus. They argue, however, that the standard should be interpreted to mean "no significant scientific disagreement." See *State Attorneys General Comments*, p. 45.

[26]As discussed above, noneconomic injury could occur if there are substitute

those claims that later research will continue to support would delay the realization of significant public health benefits. Prudence therefore dictates that, without a significant risk to consumers from a claim that reasonable scientific evidence now supports but may eventually disprove, the government should take great care to avoid prohibiting the claim. Because the FTC's concept of a reasonable basis for advertising claims explicitly considers these consequences, it is the most appropriate standard to adopt. Requiring additional evidence reflects an unwillingness to trust consumers' own choices about whether to act or to wait for government confirmation.

In its proposed rules implementing the NLEA, the FDA specifically declined to propose a definition of "significant scientific agreement." It is clear, however, both from the FDA's general discussion of the standard and from its analysis of specific claims, that the standard is high. Claims must be supported by "a sound body of scientific evidence that establishes the relationship between a substance and a particular disease."[27] Human studies "must be generalizable to, and preferably obtained from, the U.S. population."[28]

Intervention studies, in which the effects of dietary changes are evaluated prospectively in a controlled experiment, are preferred. These, of course, are the same kinds of studies that are required for approval of a new drug. The FDA acknowledges, however, that intervention studies may not be feasible in some instances, because of long latency periods or low incidence of the disease. In such circumstances, "The agency would give data from uncontrolled studies greater consideration when either scientific or ethical conditions prevent more controlled studies."[29] Despite this acknowledgment, only one of the FDA's specific decisions on the ten areas it addressed assessed the feasibility or difficulty of conducting better studies.[30] If

---

dietary changes to achieve the same objective. We discount as undocumented and wildly implausible the FDA's expressed fear that consumers who are told, for example, that diets low in cholesterol may reduce the risk of heart attack will forgo medical treatment for heart disease, choosing instead to eat more margarine. See, for example, *Federal Register*, vol. 55 (February 13, 1990), pp. 5,178–79. As discussed below, the FTC fiber study provides evidence inconsistent with the FDA's position. See the third section of this chapter.

[27]*Federal Register*, vol. 56, p. 60,548 (emphasis added).

[28]Ibid.

[29]*Federal Register*, vol. 56, p. 60,549.

[30]Claims regarding calcium and osteoporosis were tentatively approved, in part

controlled studies are feasible, they are apparently required before a health claim will be approved. If they are not feasible, they may be required anyway.

Whether "significant scientific agreement" requires more or less evidence than the "substantial evidence" required to demonstrate the safety and efficacy of new drugs is unclear. The FDA maintained in its 1990 proposal that the criteria for health messages "are not entirely dissimilar from the criteria that would be applied in substantiating the validity of a drug claim," differing primarily in the agency's willingness to consider a broader array of data for health claims.[31] That language is absent from the proposed implementing rules. The vast differences in the risks that foods and drugs pose argue strongly for a less stringent standard for foods. The statute permits such a result. Had Congress wanted to impose the same standard used for drugs, it could easily have done so.

Of course, the impact of any standard may depend more on its application than on the precise language used to define it. Significant scientific agreement is an overly restrictive standard, but less so if claims are permitted when scientists agree that diets high or low in some nutrient *may* reduce the risk of a chronic disease. Even a reasonable-basis requirement may effectively prohibit valuable information if as applied it requires additional study of well-supported but still uncertain propositions.[32]

The FDA's tentative decisions on the specific diet-disease relationships that the statute required it to address provide a further indication of how it will administer the statutory standard. The FDA tentatively approved claims in four areas: saturated fat, cholesterol, and heart disease; fat and cancer; sodium and hypertension; and calcium and osteoporosis. It tentatively decided to prohibit claims in six other areas: fiber and cancer; vitamins and cancer; fiber and heart disease; omega-3 fatty acids and heart disease; folic acid and neural tube defects; and zinc and immune function in the elderly.

---

based on recognition that truly definitive studies would take fifty or sixty years to complete. *Federal Register*, vol. 56, p. 60,697.

[31]*Federal Register*, vol. 55, p. 5,181.

[32]In some instances, the FTC has done so. See, for example, North American Phillips, 104 FTC 549 (1984), in which the commission required an additional study despite a letter from the FDA concluding that it was unnecessary.

Discerning a consistent approach in these disparate decision is difficult at best. Although some of the prohibited claims are supported by significantly less evidence than the claims the FDA approved, others are not. Indeed, it would require microscopic precision to distinguish the level of evidence for some prohibited claims from the support for other claims that the FDA would permit.

Most problematic is the FDA's tentative decision to prohibit claims about the relationship between fiber and cancer.[33] Finding a difference in the level of scientific agreement on fiber claims and other claims that the FDA would permit is difficult, if not impossible. The surgeon general's review of the evidence on nutrition and health noted that

> dietary patterns emphasizing foods high in complex carbo-hydrates and fiber are associated with lower rates of . . . some types of cancer. . . . While inconclusive, some evidence also suggests that an overall increase in intake of foods high in fiber might decrease the risk for colon cancer.[34]

The language and the conclusion are nearly identical to the surgeon general's conclusions about the relationship between fat and cancer, where the FDA would permit claims that there may be a relationship. The surgeon general concluded:

> High intake of total dietary fat is associated with increased risk for . . . some types of cancer. . . . There is substantial, although not yet conclusive, epidemiologic and animal evidence in support of an association between dietary fat intake and increased risk for cancer, especially breast and colon cancer.[35]

---

[33]The discussion that follows is also applicable to the FDA's treatment of the relationship between vitamins and cancer. The state of the evidence of a relationship is similar, there is widespread consensus that the evidence supports the prudence of increasing the role of fruits and vegetables in the diet, and the FDA's rationale for prohibiting claims is similar. For convenience, we focus on fiber. Our analysis is also relevant to claims about the relationship between fiber and heart disease. Evidence for the other claims that the FDA tentatively rejected appears to be weaker than that for the approved claims, or for the fiber and vitamin claims that it rejected.

[34]*The Surgeon General's Report of Nutrition and Health* (1988), p. 12.

[35]Ibid., p. 10.

Finding a distinction in the level of evidence in support of the relationship of fat and fiber with cancer seems to require an inordinate amount of regulatory hairsplitting. Although the FDA raises criticisms of the fiber evidence, as discussed below, it offers no principled basis for concluding that the "inconclusive" evidence of the relationship between fat and cancer is sufficient to support a claim, but the similar "not yet conclusive" evidence about fiber is not.

Even if the scientific evidence about the role of fiber remains inconclusive, the dietary implications of that evidence are almost unanimously recognized. The surgeon general,[36] the National Cancer Institute,[37] the Department of Agriculture (USDA)-Department of Health and Human Services (DHHS) dietary guidelines, and the Public Health Service all recommend increased consumption of fiber-containing foods. Increased consumption of such foods is a specific risk-reduction objective of the DHHS.[38] Even the FDA indicates that it "has supported and continues to support these recommendations and to encourage dietary guidance consistent with the recommendations."[39] Apparently, however, the FDA's support does not extend to allowing food labels to explain the reason for the recommendation.

The stated reason for the FDA's tentative decision to prohibit fiber claims is that the available evidence does not allow a determination of exactly what property of diets high in fiber reduces the risk of cancer.[40] Such diets, for example, are often low in fat and calories. Moreover, fiber-rich foods contain a variety of other nutrients, which may be the source of their protective benefits. Finally, the FDA notes there are a variety of fibers, which differ in particle size, water-holding capacity, and chemical composition. Commonly used analytical methodologies do not detect many of these characteristics, any of which may be relevant to their biological function.

The FDA's approach to claims about the relationship between fiber and cancer thus suggests a druglike approach to the assessment

---

[36]Ibid., p. 13.

[37]Quoted in ibid., p. 192.

[38]Department of Health and Human Services, Public Health Service, *Healthy People 2000: National Health Promotion and Disease Prevention Objectives* (1990).

[39]*Federal Register*, vol. 56, p. 60,576.

[40]Ibid.

of health claims. Indeed, it is hard to imagine evidence that would resolve the FDA's doubts short of one or more well-controlled clinical trials in which supplementation with a highly specific type of fiber is compared with a placebo. Any other evidence would allow the possibility that something other than fiber, or some specific attribute of the fiber that was not measured, caused the relationship. Moreover, despite the FDA's general claim that it would consider the feasibility of obtaining better evidence in assessing health claims, there is no discussion of the obvious difficulties of controlled clinical trials in the FDA's tentative decision to reject fiber claims.[41]

The FDA's attempted distinction between fiber-rich foods and fiber itself presents at least two problems. First, some of the same ambiguity is present in assessing the evidence relating fat with cancer, as low-fat diets are also higher in fiber. Indeed, the surgeon general's assessment of the relationship between fat and cancer concluded that "more precise conclusions about the role of dietary fat await the development of improved methods to distinguish among the contributions of the high-calorie, high-fat, and low-fiber components of current American dietary patterns."[42] That uncertainty is a good reason to limit claims about the relationship between fat and cancer to claims that there "may" be a relationship, which was the FDA's solution in that case. It is not a reason to prohibit claims entirely.

Second, the FDA's distinction is relevant only given a particular conception of the claim. If the claim is that "foods rich in fiber may reduce the risk," the particular characteristic of the food responsible for that effect is irrelevant. The FDA recognizes this possibility, and it specifically solicits comment on whether it should allow claims that "diets high in fruit, vegetables, and whole grains are associated with a reduced risk of cancer of the lower bowel and cardiovascular disease."[43]

---

[41]There are more express indications of the need for drug-type studies in the FDA's discussion of other rejected claims. Its discussion of omega-3 fatty acids, for example, which are possibly linked to reducing the risk of heart disease, notes that "the most compelling type of evidence to support a diet-disease relationship is a prospective, double-blinded, placebo-controlled intervention study, using CHD morbidity and mortality as endpoints." *Federal Register*, vol. 56, p. 60,672. Again, there is no acknowledgment of the obvious difficulties of conducting such a study.

[42]*Surgeon General's Report*, p. 10.

[43]*Federal Register*, vol. 56, p. 60,577.

The FDA was not, however, willing to propose this solution. In part, the FDA expresses doubt about its statutory authority to do so, because the NLEA speaks only about claims concerning the relationship of a particular nutrient to a disease. Clearly, however, the FDA had the authority to permit health claims even in the absence of the NLEA, and it twice proposed to do so. Nothing in the NLEA prohibits other claims about diseases that do not tie the disease to a specific nutrient, or suggests that Congress intended to do so.[44] Such claims should be permissible under the Food, Drug, and Cosmetics Act (FDCA) if they are not misleading. FDA need only acknowledge that they are not.

If the FDA's tentative decision stands, the Kellogg fiber campaign, developed in cooperation with the National Cancer Institute, would again be prohibited. The original FDA staff position that All-Bran cereal with health information on the box should be seized as a misbranded drug would be vindicated. It is difficult to find any other consistent reason why the FDA reached the decision it did, and hard to imagine a better illustration of the wisdom of the constitutional protection of truthful commercial speech.

In any event, properly interpreted, the operation of the statute itself should create at least some pressure for a less restrictive standard for health claims than for drugs. Health claims are prohibited, without specific findings that they would "assist consumers" for any product containing any nutrient in an amount that "increases" the risk of disease.[45] Once it has determined that a nutrient increases the risk, the FDA could hardly argue that health claims based on the absence of the nutrient were not supported by "significant scientific agreement." Indeed, significant scientific agreement that the absence

---

[44]The FDA also expresses concern that there is uncertainty about precisely which fiber characteristics may affect the risk, and hence about appropriate measurements. That uncertainty, however, has not prevented the FDA from specifying fiber measurements for required nutritional labeling or from defining "high" fiber as a nutrient descriptor. The uncertainty is just enough to prevent explaining to consumers *why* the specific quantitative information is on the label. In sharp contrast, the FDA simply dismissed the controversy over which particular saturated fatty acids contribute to heart disease risk in setting qualifying levels for claims about the relationship between saturated fat and heart disease. See *Federal Register*, vol. 56, p. 60,739.

[45]FDCA, section 403 (r) (3) (A) (ii). Disclosure of nutrients that "increase" the risk is also required for content claims about desirable nutrients.

of a nutrient may reduce risk, which is the nature of most health claims, presumably emerges long before it is possible to conclude that the nutrient does increase risk. Properly applied, the statute should allow health claims about nutrients whose presence would not be enough to bar other health claims, because the evidence would not support the conclusion of an actual increase in risk.

More important, the two standards take at least some advantage of regulatory conservatism. Particularly in the drug area, the FDA has traditionally required disclosure of negative information such as possible side effects based on far less evidence than it would require to support an affirmative claim. If it wishes to pursue a policy of "when in doubt, disclose" with regard to health-related messages, the agency must also permit affirmative health claims concerning those same nutrients.

Unfortunately, the FDA's tentative decisions are inconsistent with this portion of the statute. The FDA has proposed that products with "too much" fat, saturated fat, cholesterol, or sodium cannot make health claims of any sort. Consistent with the statutory scheme, it would permit health claims regarding each of these nutrients: that is, saturated fat or cholesterol and heart disease, fat and cancer, and sodium and hypertension.[46] For fat in particular, however, the FDA's discussion of the particular claims makes plain that fat does not meet the statutory standard as a nutrient that "increases . . . the risk of a disease."[47] In discussing the relationship between fat and heart disease, the FDA states that "while total fat is not directly linked to

---

[46]The proposed regulations clearly permit claims that reduced saturated fat and reduced cholesterol "will" reduce the risk of heart disease. Sodium claims are more ambiguous. Claims are limited to stating that a low sodium diet "is associated with or related to lower blood pressure in some people." Proposed 21 CFR 101.74 (c) (2). Such a claim seems less than a claim that sodium increases hypertension. Manufacturers apparently have the option, however, of reporting the FDA's conclusion in section (b) of the regulation that "Estimates suggest that . . . lower lifetime intake of sodium would correspond to a reduction in mortality rates of approximately 16 percent for coronary heart disease and 23 percent for stroke." With such a statement, it seems likely that consumers would interpret the claim as a statement that reducing sodium will reduce the risk. Consistency with the statutory standards requires that the FDA either permit claims that reducing sodium "will" reduce risk or eliminate sodium as a disqualifying nutrient, thereby allowing other health claims regardless of sodium content.

[47]FDCA, section 403 (r) (3) (A) (ii).

increased risk of coronary heart disease (CHD), it *may* have significant indirect effects."[48]

Moreover, the only permitted health claims involving lipids and heart disease are claims about cholesterol and saturated fat, not total fat.[49] In considering the relationship between fat and cancer, the FDA is quite explicit that the only permissible health claims are those "stated using words such as 'may' or 'might' in accordance with the strength of the evidence for the relationship."[50] Quite simply, the FDA's conclusions about specific health claims make clear that it has not determined that products high in fat "increase" the risk of either disease. Instead, the FDA based its determination of disqualifying levels of total fat on the existence of dietary recommendations that consumers should limit fat consumption to 30 percent of total calories.

The Chimera of "Perfect" Foods. Unlike the decisions of the states, the congressional decision to permit at least some health claims for foods reflects a willingness to use the competitive process to educate consumers. Because consumers want information about the relationship between diet and disease, food manufacturers have incentives to provide the information. In turn, consumer responses will generate incentives for manufacturers to improve their products, further benefiting consumers. Unfortunately, the FDA has attempted to channel the competitive process in ways likely to reduce the benefits of health claims. In particular, the FDA's implementing regulations would restrict health claims to so-called perfect foods: that is, those that do not contain significant amounts of "bad" nutrients. Although the statute itself seems to favor perfect foods, the FDA has gone far beyond the statutory requirements in its proposed rules.

A sound regulatory policy must distinguish two cases. In the first, some foods contain negative attributes that are relevant to the disease that a health claim might address. A margarine or cooking

---

[48]*Federal Register*, vol. 56, p. 60,739 (emphasis added).

[49]Because the FDA focused its review primarily on saturated fat and cholesterol, it is possible that it simply did not consider a claim about total fat and heart disease. If so, petitions for such claims should be approved.

[50]Proposed 21 CFR 101.73 (b) (4) (ii), *Federal Register*, vol. 56, p. 60,789.

oil might, for example, claim to have no cholesterol, and might note that low-fat, low-cholesterol diets reduce the risk of heart disease. Yet the product is all fat, and it contains some saturated fat, which increases the risk of heart disease.[51] In such instances, the relevant question is whether the food as a whole is consistent with the health claim. If the effects of the negative attributes are great enough that the food as a whole, used in place of likely alternatives, increases the risk of the disease it is claimed to help prevent, a health claim about that disease is clearly inappropriate. The issue, however, is a quantitative one about the effects of negative attributes, not a qualitative question of their mere presence.[52]

In the second case, products have nutritional features that reduce the risk of one disease but contain another nutrient that increases a different risk. Cheese products, for example, are relatively high in both saturated fat, which increases the risk of heart disease, and calcium, which may reduce the risk of osteopororis.[53] Restricting health claims to so-called perfect foods would prohibit claims that truthfully inform consumers about cheese products' nutritional advantages.

---

[51]Diet affects the risk of heart disease through the level of serum cholesterol. Reducing cholesterol in the diet reduces serum cholesterol, reducing the risk of heart disease. The composition of fatty acids that make up "fat" also influences serum cholesterol levels. Based on chemical differences, fatty acids are classified as saturated, monounsaturated, or polyunsaturated. There is widespread agreement that dietary saturated fat (which is solid at room temperature) increases serum cholesterol. Indeed, the magnitude of the effect of saturated fat on serum cholesterol is greater than the effect of dietary cholesterol. Polyunsaturated fat, and probably monounsaturated fat, reduces serum cholesterol levels. Different fats and oils differ significantly in their fatty acid composition, and hence in their effect on heart disease risk. See *Surgeon General's Report*, p. 10.

[52]Disclosure of the presence of negative nutrients on the nutrition label is a sensible policy, but if the food as a whole provides the benefit it claims, it is difficult to see much value in disclosures that require repeating the information somewhere else on the package.

[53]The statutory restriction applies to any claim about a disease or a "health-related condition." FDCA, section 403 (r) (1) (B). If strong bones are a health-related condition, the statute would also prohibit claims for many dairy products that calcium is important for developing strong bones in growing children, and any such claim would have to go through the elaborate petition process discussed above. Moreover, the nutrient-descriptor provisions of the statute would require the claim that a dairy product is a good source of calcium to be accompanied by a disclosure to "see the side panel for information about fat and other nutrients."

Rather than encouraging the provision of truthful information, the FDA's approach seeks to restrict health claims to so-called perfect foods. The FDA first concludes that four nutrients—total fat, saturated fat, cholesterol, and sodium—increase the risk of disease.[54] The problem then is how to determine whether an individual food contains these nutrients "in an amount which increases to persons in the general population the risk of a disease or health-related condition which is diet-related, taking into account the significance of the food in the total daily diet."[55] The FDA concedes there is no indication in the legislative history regarding what amount would increase risk, and no other basis for making such a determination:

> There are no generally recognized levels at which these nutrients in an individual food pose an increased risk of disease. Thus, FDA knows of no established or accepted approach for identifying disqualifying levels for these nutrients.[56]

Indeed, the FDA would limit any health claim to describing the effects of a particular nutrient "as part of a total dietary pattern," because, it maintains, the evidence will only support claims about dietary patterns.[57]

The FDA's specific findings lead unavoidably to the conclusion that the amounts of nutrients *in individual foods* do not increase risk. A sensible interpretation of the statute would therefore limit the prohibition to foods that, as a whole, are inconsistent with the claim. A food with enough saturated fat to increase serum cholesterol, despite its low cholesterol if used instead of likely substitutes, can

---

[54]As discussed above, it is doubtful that the agency's more specific findings about total fat support this conclusion.

[55]FDCA, section 403 (r) (3) (A) (ii).

[56]*Federal Register*, vol. 56, p. 60,543.

[57]Ibid., p. 60,551. Similarly, in deciding to evaluate the accuracy of health claims for dietary supplements under the same standard that is specified for health claims for foods, the agency concluded that "ultimately, however, it is the nutrient content of the diet that is significant, not its source." *Federal Register*, vol. 56, p. 60,540. The NLEA gave the FDA discretion to adopt a different standard for health claims for dietary supplements than the "significant scientific agreement" standard that the act specified for foods. FDCA, section 403 (r) (5) (D).

sensibly be said to increase risk because the substitution leads to a *diet* that increases risk. The absolute amounts of the "bad" nutrients in the food in question, however, are irrelevant. For nutrients relevant to a different disease, claims would be barred only if likely substitutes were superior on both disease dimensions.

That, however, was not the result the FDA reached. Instead it proceeded to invent a highly restrictive system to define the amount of nutrients in an individual food that it would regard as increasing risk. The FDA assumed that ten of the twenty food servings in the daily diet would contain the nutrient. It then considered whether to set the criterion for an amount that increases risk at 10 percent, 15 percent, or 20 percent of the recommended daily consumption of the nutrient, and it examined which foods would qualify for health claims under each standard. The 10 percent level would disqualify "a number of foods thought to be useful in maintaining a balanced diet," and the 20 percent level would permit health claims for some foods "that should not be consumed frequently in a healthy diet, including some shortenings and candies." It therefore concluded that the 15 percent level was most reasonable.[58]

To say the least, this result is arbitrary. Its rationale is that it includes foods that the FDA thinks should be included and excludes foods that it thinks should not be included. By itself, however, the 15 percent criterion would allow health claims for foods that have low amounts of the condemned nutrients solely because they have small serving sizes, even though they have a high concentration of the nutrient. To avoid this result, the FDA's proposal requires the foods to meet the 15 percent threshold per 100 grams, as well as per serving. This requirement was added because "the agency believes that nutrient-dense foods like these should not be promoted for

---

[58]*Federal Register*, vol. 56, p. 60,544. Thus, foods are disqualified if they have more than 11.5 grams of fat, 4.0 grams of saturated fat, 45 milligrams of cholesterol, or 360 milligrams of sodium. These amounts are calculated per serving, per reference amount, and per 100 grams. The "reference amount" is the standardized serving, but products in single serving packages may have a different labeled serving size. If the standardized serving size for potato chips is one ounce, for example, any package weighing less than two ounces would constitute a single serving. These disqualifying levels would also trigger requirements to disclose condemned nutrients in close proximity to claims about the content of any other nutrient under the nutrient-descriptor regulations.

increased use in a diet because they do not conform to national guidelines and that these foods should not bear health claims."[59]

This rationale, however, is inconsistent with the basis for the 15 percent calculation in the first place, which already accounts for the possibility of small serving sizes consumed frequently. If half the servings in a typical daily diet contain fat, for example, as the FDA assumes, there is no need for a further adjustment because some individual servings were small and the food was consumed on several occasions. The initial calculation already contemplates the possibility that frequent consumption of certain foods will contain enough of the nutrient to justify banning health claims about other nutrients.[60]

The FTC staff examined the impact of the FDA's proposed criteria on a data base of some 2,100 foods in twenty-seven categories.[61] If the criteria really do identify foods that increase the risk of disease, the American diet is incredibly dangerous. Indeed, there are only four categories in which more than half the foods are "safe" in that they do not increase the risk of disease—yogurt (73 percent safe); jams, jellies, and sweet sauces (93 percent safe); vegetables, fruit, and legumes (83 percent safe); and coffee, tea, soft drinks, and alcoholic beverages (99 percent safe). All poultry, meat, lunch meat, pies, nuts, and nut butters "increase risk," along with 99 percent of fish and 91 percent of ready-to-eat cereals.[62]

It is apparent from these results that the FDA's proposed criteria bear little relationship to the statutory standard that health claims are prohibited if the food contains nutrients in an amount that increases risk. Part of the problem is the 100-gram criterion, which disqualifies many foods that are a perfectly sensible part of a diet that conforms to dietary guidelines. The 100-gram criterion eliminated 60 percent of ready-to-eat cereals (100 grams = 3.5 cups), for

---

[59]*Federal Register*, vol. 56, p. 60,544.

[60]The starting point for the initial calculation is the assumption that half of the twenty servings in a typical daily diet contain fat and half contain sodium. If this assumption is correct, it makes no difference whether the ten servings containing fat, for example, include several servings of a single nutrient-dense food or ten distinct foods. The permissible amount of fat per serving is the same.

[61]The FTC data base was all food items eaten by at least one woman, aged nineteen–fifty, in the USDA's 1986 National Food Consumption survey.

[62]Ibid., p. 61.

example, along with 63 percent of breads (100 grams = four slices) and 70 percent of cream and substitutes (100 grams = seven tablespoons).

Even without that criterion, however, health claims would be prohibited for some recommended dietary changes: for example, to substitute fish and poultry for red meat.[63] Moreover, the substantial consumption levels implicit in the 100-gram criterion are hardly consistent with the statutory requirement to evaluate risk, "taking into account the significance of the food in the total daily diet."[64] Indeed, the average user of cereal consumes only about 20 grams daily; the average bread user consumes only about 35 grams.[65]

The FDA maintains that it does not intend its disqualifyng levels to create a good food–bad food concept:

> Rather, a health claim on a food label is a promise to consumers that including the food in a diet, along with other dietary modifications, will be helpful in attaining the claimed benefit and will not introduce a risk of another disease or health-related condition.[66]

We do not disagree that health claims promise that a food will be a helpful part of a diet to reduce a particular risk. That view, however, points to a substantially different regulatory approach. Claims should be permitted as long as the product, taken as a whole, used in place of likely alternatives, does indeed reduce the risk. It is far more difficult, however, to see a health claim as implying that a product has no nutritional drawbacks. The fact that individual foods do not contain nutrients in levels that, by themselves, increase risk argues strongly that claims should not be prohibited based on the effect on other diseases.[67] Dairy products, for example, should be permitted

---

[63]Ibid.

[64]FDCA, section 403 (r) (3) (A) (ii).

[65]Popkin et al., *Consumption Trends of U.S. Women*, p. 1,312. The *only* categories for which the average user consumes 100 grams per day are milk (largely because of its high water content) and grain-based mixed dishes (104 grams). The average user of pasta, rice, and cooked cereal consumes 81 grams per day; all other categories are less than 70 grams per day.

[66]*Federal Register*, vol. 56, p. 60,544.

[67]Of course, if an individual food contains levels of a nutrient that by itself increased risk, required disclosure of the risk is sensible. Even in this case, however, there is little reason to ban the claim.

to inform consumers of the fact that they are good sources of calcium and that calcium reduces the risk of osteoporosis, even though they contain fat. At most, the presence of fat should be disclosed, as it is on the nutrition label.

The disqualifying criteria are not the only requirements that restrict health claims to so-called perfect foods in the FDA proposal. There are additional restrictions on the foods eligible to make each claim. To make a claim about the relationship between fat and heart disease, for example, a product must have less than 3 grams of fat, 20 milligrams of cholesterol, and 1 gram of saturated fat per 100 grams, and it must have less than 15 percent of its calories from saturated fat.

The failure of the FDA's proposed regulatory strategy is perhaps best illustrated by examining the diet that would result if all eligible products made claims and consumers chose products based solely on health claims. These assumptions are extreme, but the FDA's approach to disqualifying levels assumes that each food eligible to make a claim should fit with a healthy diet. Comparing the resulting diet to the recommendations is thus a reasonable way to assess the impact of the FDA's approach.

Table 5–1 examines such a diet. It indicates the percentage distribution of foods considering only claims about fat and heart disease, as well as the diet that would result from the same choices if all the health claims that the FDA has tentatively approved were made.

Although commendably high in fruits and vegetables, these menus are hardly anyone's idea of the healthy diet for the average American. They include no meats. They are 3 to 5 percent candy and frozen desserts. They are low in the grain products—7 percent—that current recommendations say should form the base of a healthy diet, and low in dairy products—2 to 4 percent—even when calcium claims are considered. Both diets include a large amount of beverages, which qualify for health claims because they have no "bad" nutrients and virtually no nutrients beyond calories. Using the FDA's estimate of twenty servings per day, the diet that resulted from making food choices in the same proportion as health claims assuming all products made all permitted claims would be ten servings of vegetables, five servings of beverages, and one serving each of jams and jellies, pasta, milk, and frozen dessert. One serving would

TABLE 5–1
DIET IMPLIED BY PERMITTED HEALTH CLAIMS
(percent of diet)

Category	Fat/CHD[a]	All Claims[b]
Vegetables, fruit, legumes	58	52
Coffee, tea, soft drinks, alcoholic beverages	23	24
Jams, jellies, sweet sauces	4	5
Pasta, rice, cooked cereal	4	4
Candy	2	2
Bread	2	2
Milk	2	3
RTE cereal	1	1
Frozen desserts, pudding	1	3
Yogurt	0	1
Crackers, salty snacks	0	1

NOTE: The number of claims in each category is calculated as the number of food items in the category times the percentage of foods eligible to make a claim, expressed as a percentage of the total number of claims, rounded to the nearest 1 percent.
a. Coronary heart disease. Based on products eligible to make claims about the relationship between fat and heart disease.
b. Based on products eligible to make any of the four tentatively approved claims.
SOURCE: Based on data from FTC Comment, table 8, p. 63.

remain, to be chosen from some other category.

It is readily apparent to any casual observer of the marketplace that the distribution of products that actually make health claims differs radically from the distribution of products that would be eligible under the FDA's proposed restrictions. The reason lies in the structure of the incentives that face food marketers. These incentives derive in part from the fact that consumers want to keep eating their favorite foods. Indeed, surveys show that for many consumers, unwillingness to give up favorite foods is a major reason for not choosing a healthier diet.[68]

When new nutritional information emerges, it is likely to affect

---

[68]See the American Dietetic Association, *Survey of American Dietary Habits* (1991), p. 12, cited in FTC Comment p. 3.

certain products disproportionately. Information about the health risks of cholesterol or saturated fat, for example, has its primary impact on fat products. Because consumers interested in the recommendation will likely seek to alter their consumption of fat products, it is the producers of likely substitutes who have a powerful incentive to provide information. Likely substitutes, however, will be similar in many respects to the product with the disadvantage, differing in ways that are preferable in light of the health information.

Indeed, the desire of consumers to keep eating their favorite foods will encourage both marketers and consumers to seek products that are as similar as possible. Margarine, for example, is a good substitute for butter in the face of growing evidence about the health risks of saturated fat and cholesterol. It serves the same dietary function, but with less of the health disadvantage. Margarine producers therefore have an incentive to inform consumers of their advantage, and an incentive to improve their products in ways consistent with the health evidence. However much the FDA might wish otherwise, vegetables are simply not good substitutes for butter, and sellers of vegetables have little incentive to provide information about the health drawbacks of butter.

Based on the health risks of diets high in saturated fat and cholesterol, competition among producers of margarines, oils, and, more recently, lower-fat margarine alternatives has done much to improve the options available to consumers to reduce their risks, even though the products contain significant amounts of total fat.[69] Because such products are likely to remain significant components of the diets of most people, preserving incentives to improve them is important. Incentives for incremental improvement are particularly important given consumers' reluctance to make more radical dietary changes. The FDA recognized the importance of these incentives in deciding not to prohibit cholesterol content claims based on the product's total fat content.[70] Its proposed restrictions on health

---

[69]Margarine and butter are essentially all fat. Margarine, however, has no cholesterol and less saturated fat than butter. New margarine alternatives, which are marketed as "spreads" because they do not have enough fat to meet the regulatory definition of margarine, have less total fat as well. Although some saturated fat is essential in such products if they are to remain solid at room temperature, newer products often have lower levels of saturated fat (and higher levels of polyunsaturated fat) than older ones.

[70]*Federal Register*, vol. 56, pp. 60,496, 60,510. Total fat must be disclosed in close

claims, however, remove the ability to use food labels to provide consumers the information that would motivate them to make different choices.

The incentive problem is also relevant to products containing unrelated negative nutrients. Most foods have advantages and disadvantages. When new nutritional information comes to light, such as the importance of calcium in preventing osteoporosis, the products with the greatest incentive to provide that information to consumers are the products that inherently provide a good source of that nutrient. Producers of fats and oils, for example, but not of other products, have invested substantially to inform consumers about the benefits of modified-fat diets. Dairy products, as the leading source of calcium in most people's diets, have the greatest incentive to provide information about osteoporosis. That incentive is increased when consumption is declining because of concern about the product's negative attributes.

Rather than encouraging this process of providing information to consumers, the FDA's proposal in many instances prohibits it. Only 23 percent of milk products would be eligible for osteoporosis-prevention claims, along with 73 percent of yogurts.[71] Although lower-fat milk products can conceivably make osteoporosis-prevention claims, they are more likely to emphasize the attribute that differentiates the product—its fat content—than attributes shared with all other dairy products.

Even for products that can legally make claims, the FDA's proposal reduces the incentive to do so. Each of the tentatively approved claims is permitted only with various disclosures, some quite extensive. There is little consistency, however, in the kinds of information required. Claims about sodium and hypertension or about calcium and osteoporosis must identify the particular populations at risk, but claims about fat and cancer or fat and coronary heart disease need not do so. Sodium and calcium claims must also

---

proximity to the claim if it exceeds 11.5 grams per serving or per 100 grams. Claims are prohibited if saturated fat exceeds 2 grams per serving, a level that is less restrictive than the agency had proposed prior to the NLEA (2 grams per serving *and* less than 6 percent saturated fat on a dry weight basis). See *Federal Register*, vol. 55 (July 19, 1990), p. 29,456.

[71]The only other products that could make such claims are 2 percent of frozen desserts and puddings and 2 percent of beverages. FTC Comment, p. 63.

disclose other risk-reducing steps, but claims about fat need not do so. Claims about coronary heart disease (CHD) or osteoporosis must identify the mechanism of action, but other claims need not. Claims about CHD must indicate that not everyone will benefit, although the claim can state that "most" benefit, and sodium claims must indicate that only some will benefit; but calcium claims and fat and cancer claims are not subject to such a requirement. The model health claims that result range from thirty-one words, pertaining to fat and cancer, to seventy-six words, pertaining to calcium and osteoporosis.[72]

For any new nutrition information, the incentive problem is compounded by the need for prior regulatory review. If traditional products cannot make health claims, then fortified or modified products may be able to do so. Such products, however, are likely to be new products, rather than ones already on the market.[73] Yet before manufacturers of such potential products can provide the information that would give consumers a reason to buy, they must first go through an elaborate FDA rulemaking proceeding to authorize the claim. The costs and uncertainties of doing so are likely to constitute a substan-

---

[72]The FDA maintains, in general, that the disclosures are required by section 403 (r) (3) (B) (iii) of the statute, which provides that the regulations shall require claims to meet three criteria: the claim must be "an accurate representation of" the relationship to the disease and the significance of the nutrient, and must be stated "so that the claim enables the public to comprehend the information provided in the claim and to understand the relative significance of such information in the context of a total daily diet." The first clause requires only accuracy, not completeness. The requirement that the claim enable the public to comprehend seems primarily to require the FDA to use everyday language rather than scientific precision. Ensuring that consumers understand the relative significance of the claim may require some disclosure, but it hardly requires information about the mechanism of action or the specific risk factors for the disease. At the very least, the wide range of disclosures the FDA proposes to require shows that the agency has considerable discretion.

[73]Citrus Hill, for example, a calcium-fortified orange juice product, was introduced shortly after advertising began addressing the link between calcium and osteoporosis. More generally, the BE Fiber Study, p. 42, found that the increase in the average fiber content of new cereals was significantly higher than the average content level of older products. Similarly, new products have provided an important part of the movement to lower average tar and nicotine content of cigarettes. See Joseph Mulholland, "Policy Issues Concerning the Promotion of Less Hazardous Cigarettes," mimeo, pp. 20–21, presented at American Marketing Association Conference on Marketing and Public Policy, August 1990.

tial barrier to entry. If no one enters, no one will provide the information to consumers.

Clearly, disclosure of the presence of negative attributes in the product's nutritional labeling is an appropriate requirement. Once the information is readily available to consumers, however, it is difficult to see why they should be prohibited from learning additional important information about the health characteristics of the product from the label. That, however, is the effect of the FDA's tentative decisions to date.

Even assuming the validity of the FDA's approach to determining the amount of a nutrient that increases risks, the statute does not require restricting health claims to so-called perfect foods. The NLEA authorizes the agency to allow health claims for products with negative attributes "based on a finding that such a claim would assist consumers in maintaining healthy dietary practices,"[74] provided that the negative attributes and a reference to the nutrition label are prominently disclosed in immediate proximity to the health claim.[75] An identical finding is required to permit truthful claims that a product is "cholesterol-free" if the product contains levels of fat or saturated fat that increase the risk of disease and does not usually contain cholesterol.[76]

Wisely, the FDA has tentatively decided to permit "no-cholesterol" claims even on products that are high in fat.[77] Based on

[74]FDCA, section 403 (r) (3) (A) (ii). There is no apparent basis for the statutory presumption that truthful information about the positive characteristics of a product that also has negative attributes will *not* assist consumers. Absent such a basis, however, it is difficult to see how the presumption can survive constitutional challenge as an undue restriction on truthful commercial speech. The congressional recognition that such claims can assist consumers rules out an argument that the claims are inherently deceptive, and it is difficult to imagine how the claim is deceptive if the negative attribute is disclosed. Nonetheless, such claims are prohibited until FDA rules.

[75]Given that virtually all consumers are presumably aware that nutrition labels exist, and they can easily find out about the negative attributes from that label, the benefits of this additional disclosure in a different portion of the package are elusive at best. Moreover, these requirements increase the cost of providing information, which reduces the incentive to do so. The far more serious problem, however, is prohibiting health claims altogether.

[76]FDCA, section 403 (r) (2) (A) (iii) (I).

[77]Additional, and sometimes extreme, disclosures are required, however. A margarine, for example, could only report that it has no cholesterol if it disclosed that it

survey evidence that consumers want and use such claims to identify appropriate foods:

> FDA believes it is helpful to consumers to highlight "cholesterol-free" foods useful in maintaining healthy dietary practices whether the food is inherently free of cholesterol or is processed to be that way.[78]

Despite this finding, the brief discussion of the statutory provision permitting health claims if they assist consumers asserts that "The agency is not, however, aware of information to support" a regulation allowing health claims about cholesterol for foods high in fat.[79]

If cholesterol-content information will assist consumers who know that cholesterol is important and seek out products that are cholesterol-free, obviously health claims explaining its significance to consumers who do *not* know would also assist consumers. Indeed, the FDA views a cholesterol-content claim as a species of health claim, even if it is not a health claim under the statute. It concluded:

> A significant number of consumers are likely to perceive that food that bears a cholesterol content claim will help to lower blood cholesterol levels and to reduce the risk of heart disease.[80]

Moreover, the proposed levels of saturated fat that would bar health claims are substantially lower than the levels that would be permitted for cholesterol-content claims, and content claims are permitted with disclosure regardless of total fat content.[81] There is no rational basis

---

"contains 100 percent less cholesterol than butter. Contains no cholesterol, compared with 30 milligrams in one serving of butter. Contains 11 grams of fat per serving." *Federal Register*, vol. 56, p. 60,505. If margarine were inherently cholesterol-free, it would only have to disclose that it contains 11 grams of fat per serving. Margarine is not inherently cholesterol free, however, because the standard of identity for margarine permits the use of animal fats, although virtually no margarines do so.

[78]*Federal Register*, vol. 56, p. 60,498.

[79]*Federal Register*, vol. 56, p. 60,544.

[80]*Federal Register*, vol. 56, p. 60,509.

[81]Health claims about the relationship between cholesterol or saturated fat and heart disease are prohibited if the product contains more than 1 gram of saturated fat per 100 grams. *Federal Register*, vol. 56, p. 60,747. Cholesterol content claims are permitted as long as the product contains less than 2 grams of saturated fat per serving. *Federal Register*, vol. 56, p. 60,505.

for treating explicit health claims any differently.

The evidence would support a finding that all health claims would "assist consumers" as long as the product as a whole, as part of an otherwise sensible diet, reduces the risk of the disease that the claim concerns. Certainly, the FDA should make such a finding for claims linking cholesterol content of fats and oils with heart disease prevention, and for claims linking calcium content of dairy products with osteoporosis prevention.[82]

Market Outcomes versus Market Manipulation. The available evidence indicates that the unfolding process of learning health-related information one fact at a time does indeed work. Most marketing information, on labels or in advertising, has focused on cholesterol, without detailed discussion of fat or saturated fat. As a result, awareness of dietary cholesterol as a risk factor for heart disease increased from 26 percent in 1982 to 40 percent in 1986. At the same time, the belief that consumption of fats, especially saturated fats, may increase the risk of heart disease rose from 29 to 43 percent.[83] Certainly these data provide no basis to conclude that labels that highlight the effects of cholesterol are misleading.

Similarly, the evidence available to date provides no basis for concerns that health messages focusing on one attribute of a product may lead to consumer selection of products that are worse on other health-related attributes. The FTC's study of the cereal market found that after health claims began, preexisting trends toward reduced sodium and reduced fat in high-fiber cereals continued and, if anything, accelerated. Indeed, fat reduction *only* occurred among high-fiber cereals; fat content of low-fiber cereals actually increased after health claims began.[84] Thus there is no factual basis for disclosure requirements beyond the nutrition label itself or for restricting health claims to so-called perfect foods.

This evidence also undermines one of the main arguments for

---

[82]The FDA declined to allow health claims for whole milk because low fat milk and skim milk would be able to make the claim. *Federal Register*, vol. 56, p. 60,545. Although some eligible products exist, only eleven of the forty-seven "milk" products in the USDA's data base would be able to make the claims. See FTC Comment, p. 63.

[83]Blumenthal, "The Health-Diet Link," p. 23.

[84]BE Fiber Study, pp. 38–41.

government control over health information: eliminating consumer confusion. Increasing information inevitably will increase confusion, particularly when the information first appears. Ignorance is bliss. Without information, one need not think and cannot be confused. The increased use of health claims has undoubtedly increased thinking, hence confusion. Over time, however, consumers learn and act on the information. The available evidence indicates that consumers are more aware of the health benefits of what they eat and are making choices based upon that awareness. The recently enacted federal statute and the FDA's implementation of regulations, however, will curtail at least some of the benefits of health claims.

A related argument is the FDA's view that restrictions beyond those the Federal Trade Commission imposes on advertising are necessary for "maintaining order . . . in the marketplace."[85] Some states have also expressed concern over the lack of order. This view fundamentally miscomprehends markets, because it presupposes a known outcome toward which the market should proceed.

By their nature, markets are disorderly. Indeed, the competitive process has been characterized as "creative destruction."[86] New ideas, new products, and new innovations continually emerge, challenging the prevailing order. A multitude of sellers and a multitude of claims compete for consumers' attention. Each is tested by millions of consumers for its ability to satisfy their preferences. Judged in this crucible, many fail. Those that succeed provoke a new wave of rival products and claims.[87] In short, the market itself is no more orderly than the disparate and constantly changing desires of the consumers whose collective preferences it reveals.

As individuals, we may find many emergent products and claims distasteful, or even unsuitable. The market process, however, and only the market process reveals the outcomes that best satisfy consumers. For government regulators, the pragmatic approach of the Federal Trade Commission should guide decisions, recognizing the

---

[85]*Federal Register*, vol. 55 (1990), p. 5,188.

[86]Joseph A. Schumpeter, *Capitalism, Socialism, and Democracy* (N.Y.: Harper & Row, 1947).

[87]In this regard, the market process is not unlike the process of scientific debate, on which we would not think of imposing an artificial concept of "order." The metaphor of the marketplace of ideas is apt in more ways than one.

vast power of communication to educate and benefit consumers and applying a flexible, reasonable-basis test to evaluate the support for claims. Misplaced concepts of order may make the market look less chaotic, but inexorably they will reduce the benefits of competition to consumers.

One concern that led to the congressional approach is fear of the FDA's inability to enforce rules against false or misleading health messages. The agency has challenged "drug claims for health fraud products," which manufacturers defended as consistent with the FDA's 1987 health claims proposal.[88] Indeed, when the FDA lost a motion for summary judgment in just such a case because it could not distinguish the challenged claims from those it was willing to permit, it was spurred to develop its more restrictive 1990 proposal.[89] The problem in that case, however, was that the FDA apparently based its case solely on the notion that the product was a drug, given the claims made for it. The FDA did not contest the one fact that should distinguish legal claims from illegal ones—illegal claims are false or deceptive.

If the claims were false or misleading and the FDA had challenged them on those grounds, it would almost certainly have succeeded. Indeed, the Federal Trade Commission, with far less knowledge of the scientific accuracy of claims regarding diet and health, has had great success challenging fraudulent health claims in the federal courts and in administrative litigation. Based on allegations that the claims were false or deceptive, the commission has stopped claims very similar to the one that the FDA will have to try in order to win.[90] In challenging fradulent claims, the FTC has obtained temporary restraining orders, preliminary and permanent injunctions, and even ex parte asset freezes.[91] Unable to rely on the legal

---

[88]The FDA sought, for example, to challenge cholesterol reduction claims for fish oil supplements as drug claims. Whether it considered these "health fraud products" is unclear. See *Federal Register*, vol. 56, p. 60,665.

[89]United States v. U.S. Health Club, Inc., 87 Civ. 7779 (RWS), 716 F. Supp. 787 (S.D.N.Y., July 11, 1989).

[90]See, for example, Pharmtech Research, Inc., 576 F. Supp. 294 (DDC 1983) (preliminary injunction); claim that dehydrated vegetable tablet could reduce cancer risks.

[91]FTC v. Furman, 84-0803-A (E.D. Va.; filed August 6, 1984); temporary restrain-

crutch of alleging that a food has become a drug, the FTC has had to challenge misleading health claims on their merits. It has proven conclusively that doing so poses no significant hurdles.

Labeling and Advertising

By its terms, Congress's recent pronouncement affects only labeling; the differences between the Federal Trade Commission and the states regarding advertising remain unresolved. Although the statute will undoubtedly be influential, and although there are efforts to require uniformity between advertising and labels, neither sound public policy, nor logic, nor precedent requires such uniformity.[92] Whatever requirement the FDA imposes on labels, advertising regulations should, to the maximum extent possible, remain under the principles discussed in the first section of this monograph.

Regarding public policy, the basic regulatory principles discussed above remain applicable to the regulation of advertising. Information in the hands of consumers is a powerful force for effective competition. When that information is truthful and not misleading, it should not be prohibited because it is "unsuitable" or "inappropriate." Sound policy must also recognize that someone will misinterpret virtually anything, and it should not prohibit truthful claims because of the possibility of bizarre or idiosyncratic misinterpretations. Finally, sound policy must recognize that information is inevitably incomplete and that attempts to require an impossible perfection may leave consumers with no information at all. The consensus that has developed around these principles of advertising regulation should continue to apply to health claims.

Regarding logic, in applying the appropriate principles there are differences between advertising and labeling. The basic functions of the two means of conveying information differ in the typical company's marketing plans. Advertising serves to identify products that consumers with a particular interest should consider further.

---

ing order and asset freeze in sale of bogus hair analysis tests; injunction granted February 25, 1985. FTC v. H.N. Singer, Inc., 668 F.2d 1107 (9th Cir. 1982); upholding authority for asset freeze. The FTC's success in obtaining such remedies is discussed generally in the 1989 ABA Report, pp. 45–48.

[92] An example is H.R. 1662, the Nutrition Advertising Coordination Act of 1991.

Labeling serves as a source of more detailed information about uses and characteristics of the product.[93] Comprehensive ingredient labeling, for example, is useful to consumers, but ingredient advertising necessarily highlights particular ingredients: for example, made with milk, or with oat bran, or with a blend of whole grains. Consumers whose interest is attracted by advertising claims can easily obtain additional information from the label, but it does not follow that advertising should provide the same information as well.

Both costs and benefits of a particular regulatory strategy are likely to differ for advertisements and labels. Disclosures are likely to be far more costly in advertising, and particularly in broadcast advertising, than on product labels. Television time or print-advertising space are expensive; product labels are generally a cheaper location for detailed information.[94] Similarly, the FDA's prohibition on highlighting certain content information for products that exceed "disqualifying levels" of "bad" nutrients imposes lower costs in labels where the nutrition label itself provides the information.[95] In advertising, where providing comprehensive information is far more difficult, such a prohibition would mean the information must be obtained elsewhere.

As to benefits, consumers must remember information provided through advertising before they can use it. The recall problem is particularly severe, because additional information only tangentially related to an advertisement's primary message may detract from the ad's ability to communicate at all. Information on the label, however, is available for use immediately and whenever needed. Moreover, the availability of the information on the label reduces the benefits of repeating the same information in an advertisement. In short, the benefits of advertising disclosures are fewer than those of label disclosures, and the costs are higher.

---

[93]Of course, labeling also includes material that is essentially indistinguishable from advertising. It remains, however, more detailed and more comprehensive.

[94]The costs of label disclosures are hardly trivial, however. Indeed, the FDA estimates that just printing new labels to comply with the NLEA will cost $756 million. *Federal Register*, vol. 56, p. 60,865. Moreover, requiring additional information may displace other information that would be more useful to consumers.

[95]The disqualifying levels for nutrient content claims are essentially the same as the levels for health claims, and they are discussed in the second section of this chapter.

There are other differences between advertising and labeling as well. Standardizing label formats may facilitate comparison of competing products on the store shelf, while similar standardization would impair the ability to create advertising that communicates effectively. It would offer no corresponding advantage, because consumers cannot compare specific advertisements at the point of sale. In advertising, a given statement may be made in such different contexts that it conveys different meanings; the greater uniformity of labels reduces this risk. Labels and advertisements are different in ways that justify differences in treatment.[96]

Regarding precedent, marketers, the FDA, and the FTC have substantial experience with different regulatory standards governing labeling and advertising. Over-the-counter drug labeling is regulated by the FDA, but advertising is regulated by the FTC.[97] Nonetheless, the FTC has long recognized that it need not apply all FDA regulatory policies to advertising. In 1981 it unanimously rejected a proposed rule that would have required advertising for over-the-counter drugs to use only FDA-approved labeling language to describe a product's indications for use.[98] In 1984 the commission unanimously rejected a proposed rule that would have required antacid advertising to include all warnings that appear on the label.[99] Neither decision was controversial; both were supported by liberal commissioner Michael Pertschuk.

---

[96]The contention that consumers find labels more credible than advertising is not a justification for disparate treatment, even if it is correct. The kind of information on labels—ingredients, weight, nutrition labeling—is inherently more credible than advertising claims about taste, texture, and the like, precisely because the label information is objective and usually verifiable. Tony the Tiger gains no credibility when he moves from the television screen to the cereal box. The nature of the information conveyed, not the means of conveyance, leads to any difference in credibility.

[97]Some have cited prescription drugs, where FDA controls both labeling and advertising, to argue for uniform standards for health claims. See Bruce Silverglade, "A Comment on Public Policy Issues in Health Claims for Foods," *Journal of Public Policy and Marketing*, vol. 10 (1991), pp. 54, 60. Given the nature of the risks involved, however, the OTC drug analogy seems far more persuasive.

[98]*Federal Register*, vol. 46 (1981), p. 24,584. At the time, FDA required labels to use specifically approved language and prohibited any other description of indications for use. Wisely, the FDA has since abandoned that policy.

[99]*Federal Register*, vol. 49 (1984), p. 46,156.

Similarly, the commission has not universally followed FDA policies regarding food labels. In 1980, for example, it unanimously abandoned a proposed rule that would have required substantial amounts of nutrition-label information in advertising.[100] In the difference most relevant to the debate about health claims, for nearly two decades the commission has consistently refused to follow or even propose the FDA's policy regarding claims about the relationship between cholesterol and heart disease.

Until Kellogg's fiber advertising campaign forced a full review of its policy, the FDA had prohibited any mention on food labels of the relationship between cholesterol and heart disease. Indeed, the agency's willingness to allow even cholesterol content information was grudging at best. Although the NLEA will require changes, under current regulations cholesterol information on food labels is an optional part of nutrition labeling, and companies that choose to provide it must disclose that information about cholesterol is provided for the benefit of those who, on the advice of a physician, are pursuing a modified-fat diet. Nonetheless, the different standards governing cholesterol advertising and labeling did not create any significant difficulties for marketers who had to comply with both. Advertising claims not repeated on the label were common. Compared with the pre-1984 policy, the NLEA has actually increased the consistency between advertising and labeling policies.

Any lack of consistency regarding health claims creates costs for consumers, however. They are denied the ability to use labels for information. The availability of the same information on the label would reduce the risk of misunderstanding, because it would give consumers the opportunity to reread the information and to consider it at their leisure. Because information would be available through more channels of communication, a consistent policy of allowing claims that are truthful and not misleading in advertising and on labels would benefit consumers. Applying the NLEA to advertising would only increase the costs by denying certain information altogether.

The NLEA will of course create considerable pressure for the FTC to follow the FDA's determinations. The appropriate FTC response, however, depends on the specific nature of those determi-

[100]*Federal Register*, vol. 45 (1980), p. 23,705.

CONCLUSION

nations. If the FDA concludes that the evidence does not support a particular claim, FTC deference to that conclusion is appropriate, given the relative knowledge of the two agencies. The FDA may also prohibit a claim on labels, however, because there is not yet "significant scientific agreement," even if the claim is probably true. It has tentatively concluded, for example, that even though the National Cancer Institute recommends high-fiber diets, there was not yet sufficient scientific agreement to permit the claim on labels that fiber produces the desired effect. Even if the FDA decides it can permit claims only about the substance itself, the FTC can certainly allow claims about fiber-rich foods, which the FDA recognizes have wide scientific support. Or a particular claim may be prohibited on labels only because the FDA is continuing to review the evidence. In such circumstances, advertising claims that do not overstate the evidence or its significance should be permissible. The core notion of advertising policy, which the commission has consistently followed, is to provide the opportunity for both sides of a legitimate scientific controversy to make their cases to the public and allow the marketplace to choose.[101]

Health Claims—Conclusion

Since Kellogg's 1984 defiance of the FDA's prohibition on any use of food labels to inform consumers that diet and health are related, regulatory developments concerning health claims have been rapid. Applying the consensus on appropriate advertising policy discussed in part one, the FTC tolerated and even encouraged the new emphasis on health claims in advertising. Because Kellogg had the support of other parts of the Department of Health and Human Services—in particular, of the National Cancer Institute—the FDA decided not to enforce its rule. Nonetheless, the prohibition remained on the books and still commanded appreciable support.

---

[101]Thus, for example, the commission entered orders allowing margarine manufacturers to claim that "many doctors recommend" low fat, low cholesterol diets to reduce the risk of heart disease, Standard Brands, Inc., 82 FTC 1176 (1973), while also entering an order that permitted egg producers to dispute the relationship between dietary cholesterol and heart disease (provided they disclosed that there was controversy about the issue). National Commission on Egg Nutrition, 88 FTC 89 (1976), aff'd as modified, 570 F.2d 157 (7th Cir. 1977).

81

The advertising campaigns that resulted produced large benefits for consumers, as the FTC's fiber study revealed. Nevertheless, the FTC's willingness to permit a variety of advertising claims that were technically illegal on food labels, combined with the controversy about which regulatory standards should govern such claims, created an irresistible opportunity for a group of activist state attorneys general. Urging continued regulatory prohibitions, they acted against a variety of health-related advertising claims that federal authorities had implicitly or explicitly decided to permit.

The inability to adapt advertising claims to the demands of individual jurisdictions created severe difficulties for national advertisers. Faced with state standards that conflicted with and were more restrictive than federal policy, the business community supported the NLEA to impose a uniform standard for health claims on product labels. At least for food labels, the result is a single national standard, with an enhanced and untested role for state enforcement.

The resulting uniform standard is based firmly on a regulatory approach to the relationship between diet and health, relying heavily on the regulator's assessment of the most appropriate diet for consumers to follow. As with most statutes, the NLEA represented a compromise. Because the act recognizes that at least some health information should be permissible, it is distinctly preferable to the absolute prohibition that the FDA actively enforced until 1984. It is inferior, however, to the advertising policy approach of examining claims case by case to determine whether there is a reasonable basis for the conclusion.

As this chapter has detailed, the likely result is a significant delay in consumers' ability to learn about new information concerning the relationship between diet and disease from product labels. The new standard should reduce, if not eliminate, the risks of conflicting federal and state decisions, at least on labels. It does so, however, at the cost of a policy that, from the perspective of consumers, is unduly restrictive.

6
Environmental Marketing

THE CURRENT WAVE of environmental advertising is not the first. Twenty years ago, similar environmental advertising emerged.[1] It too provoked allegations of deception,[2] regulatory reactions,[3] and proposals for statutory change.[4] Whether as a result of regulatory overkill or of flagging consumer interest, advertising that focused on environmental attributes diminished substantially.

The Problem

Interest in environmental issues has been renewed over the past few years. Concern about toxic wastes, acid rain, global warming, and ozone destruction has prompted intense debate and, in some instances, statutory and regulatory responses. Concern about the environment has also been reflected in consumer demand for products that are environmentally improved.

A spate of advertising addressing environmental benefits of numerous products has resulted. Plastics, for example, have been advertised as "degradable" or "recyclable." A wider variety of products have been advertised as being made from "recycled" material or as being "recyclable." Disposable-diaper manufacturers have

---

[1]See for example, Nancy Giges, "Pollution—It's Today's Bonanza for Advertisers," *Advertising Age* (April 20, 1970), p. 1. Although some advertising concerned product attributes, a far larger fraction of environmental advertising in the 1970s was "image" advertising, focused on a company's pollution control efforts.

[2]"Corporate Advertising and the Environment," *Economic Priorities Report*, vol. 2 (September–October 1971), p. 2.

[3]An example is Standard Oil Co. of California, 84 FTC 1401 (1974).

[4]Indeed, legislation was introduced to impose prison terms of up to six months for false antipollution claims. "Spong Bill Asks Jail for False Pollution Claims," *Advertising Age* (March 1, 1971), p. 1.

sought to develop and emphasize "compostability," as have makers of plastic bags for yard waste. Manufacturers of aerosol-spray products have advertised that they do not contain ozone-depleting chlorofluorocarbons or, more simply, that they are "ozone-friendly" or "ozone-safe." Foamed plastic products have made similar claims. Many, if not most, of these claims have provoked controversy.

A key focus of the recent round of environmental advertising has been solid-waste disposal. Because of stricter regulatory standards, numerous sanitary landfills have been closed. Consequently, municipalities have faced potential shortages of future landfill capacity and sharply higher waste-disposal costs.[5] These facts, combined with well-publicized garbage shipments that could not find a final resting place, have increased public attention to the unglamorous subject of solid-waste disposal.

The saga of degradable plastics illustrates the complex interaction among public concerns, market responses, and regulatory developments. A mounting public fear that "plastic is forever," combined with concerns about the magnitude of the solid-waste disposal problem, led to an effective political demand for degradable plastics. By 1990, for example, twenty-one states required that plastic six-pack connectors be degradable; three other states imposed similar requirements by 1991.[6] Other state legislation was broader, requiring, for example, that plastic bags be degradable.[7] At one point as many as thirty-five states were considering legislation that would restrict plastic packaging in one way or another,[8] and a number of federal proposals were introduced as well.[9] In 1988 Congress enacted legis-

---

[5]The problem may be less of a lack of good sites for landfills than of local opposition to new landfills—the so-called NIMBY (not in my backyard) phenomenon.

[6]Sadun, Webster, and Commoner, *Breaking Down the Degradable Plastics Scam*, report prepared for Greenpeace (March 1990), p. 13.

[7]Examples include South Dakota (South Dakota Statute title 34A-7-5.1), banning nondegradable plastic garbage bags, beginning in 1992; Florida (Florida Statute section 403.708), requiring plastic bags from retail outlets to degrade within 120 days; Iowa (Iowa Code section 455B.301), disposable plastic bags must be degradable. The rise and fall of degradability requirements is well illustrated by Minnesota, which passed a requirement that state agencies purchase only "degradable" plastic bags, but repealed it before it went into effect. The *Green Report*, p. 31, n. 21.

[8]Jennifer Lawrence, "Mobil Case Study," *Advertising Age*, vol. 62 (January 29, 1991), p. 12.

[9]Examples include, HR 1439, Degradable Plastics Act of 1989 (Lancaster);

lation requiring the EPA to issue federal regulations requiring degradable six-pack rings within two years.[10]

Whether environmentally sound or not, the regulatory pressures
reflected consumer demand for degradable plastics, and the marketplace responded. At first, several small companies introduced degradable plastics in garbage bags and grocery bags and incorporated
degradable plastics in such other products as disposable diapers.
These products were based either on the addition of cornstarch to the
plastic mix to produce a "biodegradable" plastic or, alternatively, on
various additives to increase sensitivity to ultraviolet light, creating a
"photodegradable" product.

The success of the initial degradable products inspired imitation
by the major firms in the industry, most prominently in the production of plastic bags.[11] First Brands, the maker of Glad bags, introduced degradable bags in early 1989, and in June 1989 Mobil
Chemical followed with degradable Hefty bags. Thus in only a few
years degradable plastic bags had replaced their conventional coun-
terparts in the branded portion of the industry.[12]

Given an issue with proven political appeal, state regulators
were quick to announce their concerns about "green" claims in
general and degradability claims in particular. By late 1989, seven
states had formed a new task force to address such claims, a group
that eventually grew to eleven.[13] The state task force conducted two
days of public hearings in March 1990 and issued a preliminary
report seven months later.[14] Unlike efforts involving health claims,

---

S. 1237, Degradable Commodity Plastics Procurement and Standards Act of 1989
(Glenn).

[10]The EPA announced that it would issue proposed regulations implementing this
provision in March 1993. "Unified Agenda of Federal Regulations," *Federal Register*,
vol. 57 (April 27, 1992), p. 17,417.

[11]In other industries, notably disposable diapers, the major brands did not imitate
the small companies that introduced products made with "disposable" plastics.

[12]Hefty and Glad together account for approximately 52 percent of the market and
are the only significant nationally marketed brands. See Lawrence, "Mobil Case
Study," p. 13. The remainder of the market is primarily store brands.

[13]Jennifer Lawrence, "Attorneys General Attack 'Green' Claims," *Advertising Age*
(December 18, 1989), p. 8.

[14]Attorneys General of California, Florida, Massachusetts, Minnesota, Missouri,
New York, Texas, Utah, Washington, and Wisconsin, *The Green Report: Findings
and Preliminary Recommendations for Responsible Environmental Advertising* (No-

state activity concerning environmental claims has focused on achieving uniform federal standards, enforceable by both federal and state officials. In its preliminary report, the state task force called on the federal government to develop guidelines for environmental claims, whether at the FTC or at the Environmental Protection Agency. That call was reiterated in the final report, issued in May 1991.[15]

Nevertheless, the states have also initiated enforcement actions without waiting for federal guidelines. Most notably, seven states filed individual lawsuits challenging Mobil's degradability claims in June 1990, three months after Mobil had announced that it was abandoning the claims.[16] The heart of the states' cases was the contention that Mobil's bags would not degrade in a landfill, the destination of most trash, because landfills are designed to retard degradation of all materials. The states did not seriously dispute the package's statement that, upon exposure to sunlight, the bags would indeed degrade,[17] but they argued that the bags could not extend the life of landfills and so their degradability was irrelevant.[18]

Unlike most other national marketers confronted with state charges, Mobil resisted. Some states sought preliminary injunctions or temporary restraining orders, but none prevailed.[19] Although the Texas case was settled promptly with Mobil agreeing to halt the claims unless they conformed to federal guidelines, the other cases dragged on for a year. They were settled in June 1991, with Mobil agreeing not to make claims until federal standards were in place, and paying $25,000 to each state. In essence, the orders give the

vember 1990). Tennessee joined this group before it issued its final report in May 1991.

[15]*The Green Report II: Recommendations for Responsible Environmental Advertising* (May 1991).

[16]Lawrence, "Mobil Case Study," p. 13. Lawsuits were filed by California, Massachusetts, Minnesota, New York, Washington, Wisconsin, and Texas.

[17]See, for example, Commonwealth of Massachusetts v. Mobil Chemical Company, Inc., Superior Court Civil Action no. 90–3390, complaint para. 14–18.

[18]Mobil's package also claimed that after exposure to sunlight, the bags would continue to degrade even in a landfill. The state's theory, however, was considerably broader, arguing that any degradability claim is deceptive.

[19]Both Wisconsin and New York went to court, unsuccessfully, to enjoin preliminarily Mobil's advertising.

states the ability to enforce any federal standard that may be adopted. The money can be used only for consumer education or cooperation with the Federal Trade Commission to develop guidelines.

Another state enforcement action involving environmental claims was against American Enviro Products, Inc., over claims that its Bunnies disposable diapers were biodegradable. As in the Mobil cases, the states did not dispute that Bunnies would indeed degrade under certain conditions. Rather, they maintained that the product would not degrade in a landfill.[20] Although not formally part of the settlement, the company and the states agreed on a 750-word environmental essay to appear on the Bunnies box. The utility of such a lengthy disclosure is questionable, to say the least.

The Federal Trade Commission has also actively pursued a number of investigations of environmental advertising and labeling claims. Prodded in part by state activity, the commission is reportedly investigating similar degradability claims.[21] Although FTC investigations generally take considerably longer than typical state proceedings, cases have begun to emerge. Recently the commission, for example, announced its own consent agreement with American Enviro Products. The complaint alleged that packaging and advertising for Bunnies diapers claimed the product would offer a significant environmental benefit when disposed in a landfill; that they would completely break down in three to five years; and that they would degrade more rapidly than other disposable diapers in a landfill.[22] A similar order with First Brands covers degradability claims for trash bags.[23]

In addition to requiring evidence to support such claims in the future, the orders include a separate provision governing claims that the product is compostable. If compostability claims are made, the provision requires the company to disclose that the product is not

---

[20]In the Matter of American Enviro Products, Inc., Assurance of Discontinuance with the Attorneys General of California, Florida, Massachusetts, Minnesota, Missouri, New York, Texas, Utah, Washington, and Wisconsin (1990).

[21]Jennifer Lawrence and Steven N. Colford, "Green Guidelines Are the Next Step," *Advertising Age* (January 29, 1991), p. 28.

[22]In the Matter of American Enviro Products, Inc., et al., File no. 902 3110 (August 30, 1991); consent.

[23]In the Matter of First Brands Corp., File no. 902 3113 (January 16, 1991); consent.

designed to degrade in landfills. The order also requires the company to disclose the information that composting facilities are generally unavailable, or alternatively the percentage of the population with access to composting programs.

The provisions regulating compostability claims are not a part of the states' settlement regarding Bunnies, and the basis for their inclusion in the FTC order is not clear. These provisions are considerably more specific than traditional "fencing-in" relief, which would simply require compostability claims to satisfy a reasonable basis requirement.[24] Moreover, if compostability claims are constructed in a manner or placed in a context that gives rise to a general degradability claim, they would be subject to the order's general requirement.

A possible reason for these provisions is to provide a "safe harbor," thereby protecting the company from more restrictive state action against the claim. But disclosure that the product will not degrade in a landfill would be enough to remove the claim from the order's other provisions. The additional disclosures about composting facilities are unnecessary as a safe harbor from the FTC order, although they may provide more protection from state action. If so, the compostability provisions reflect at best a compromise with an even more restrictive state standard. Unfortunately, as discussed in more detail below, the disclosure requirements are overly restrictive. The result thus illustrates how compromises intended to avoid the procedural difficulties of multiple regulation can instead harm consumer welfare.

Moreover, the FTC has become the focus of the call for federal guidelines to regulate environmental claims. Besides the task force of state attorneys general,[25] an industry coalition of eleven trade associations led by the National Food Processors Association filed a petition asking the FTC to adopt guidelines for environmental advertising and proposing specific language for them.[26] Individual compa-

---

[24]By "fencing-in," the FTC can regulate conduct in areas in which no violation has yet occurred. Orders often apply, for example, to a broader range of products than those involved in the challenged conduct.

[25]*Green Report II.*

[26]In the matter of National Food Processors Association, Petition for Industry Guides for Environmental Claims under Section Five of the Federal Trade Commission Act (February 14, 1991).

nies and associations have filed similar petitions.[27] Even the Environmental Protection Agency joined the call for FTC guidelines.[28] The mounting pressure for FTC guides led the commission to hold two days of public hearings concerning guides in July 1991. Most participants argued that guides were needed. The commission has also established an interagency working group with the Environmental Protection Agency and the U.S. Office of Consumer Affairs to consider environmental claims.

At the moment, consumers are interested in environmental claims. In several different polls, consumers have indicated a preference for environmentally improved products and a willingness to pay more for such products.[29] Although survey evidence of willingness to pay is notoriously unreliable, apparently many consumers would choose environmentally improved products.

Beyond the problems of survey evidence, however, consumer interest in environmentally conscientious product attributes may not be significant. Individuals who pay more for an environmental attribute bear all the costs, but their contribution to environmental improvement is trivial. Moreover, the benefits of that improvement are widely shared by consumers who make choices based purely on private concerns. This externality problem, which provides the intellectual rationale for environmental regulation, also suggests that most consumers are unlikely to incur significant costs for environmental benefits.[30]

Nonetheless, significant numbers of consumers are currently

---

[27]An example is the Petition for Federal Trade Commission Guides on Environmental Claims, submitted by Mobil Chemical Company (September 12, 1990).

[28]Address by William K. Reilly to the National Press Club, Washington, D.C., September 26, 1990, p. 13.

[29]In one survey, for example, 88 percent of consumers reported a willingness to pay more for environmentally safe products. Scott Hume and Patricia Stenad, "Consumers Go Green," *Advertising Age* (September 25, 1989), p. 3. In another survey, a New York design and marketing firm found that 78 percent of consumers would pay up to 5 percent more for environmentally sound containers; 47 percent would pay 15 percent more. Gerstman and Meyers, Inc., *Consumer Solid Waste: Awareness Attitude and Behavior Study II* (July 1990). In a Roper poll, consumers reported willingness to pay an average of 6.6 percent more for environmentally sound products. *Environmental Report* (BNA) (August 3, 1990) p. 691.

[30]Of course, if the government *requires* certain attributes, such as recyclability, consumers will not have a choice.

willing to incur some costs for environmental benefits. Recycling programs have prospered, for example, even though they usually require individuals to sort and deliver the material. Some environmental improvements may not impose appreciable additional costs. Degradable plastic bags, for example, were introduced without price increases, and although the claims have largely ceased, the degradant additives are apparently still in use. To the extent that consumers care, the market retains its ability to address their concern with specific product improvements, provided the regulatory system permits it to do so.[31]

Approaches to Environmental Claims

Two conceptual approaches to regulating environmental claims have been suggested. Under the first, the environmental regulation approach, the first step is to determine the "proper" environmental policy. Often this step is implicit rather than explicit. Definitions of terms and restrictions on claims are then structured to permit claims that advance the desired policy and to prohibit or restrict claims that do not. If degradability, for example, does not facilitate solutions to solid-waste problems because landfills retard degradation and because recycling should be encouraged to reduce use of landfills, then degradability claims should be restricted.

In essence, the environmental regulation approach seeks to control the flow of information to consumers, thus manipulating choices to achieve "desirable" market outcomes. Although it uses market mechanisms, it is based on the paternalistic judgment that if certain choices are environmentally sound, then consumers should make them. To justify using this approach in enforcing statutory restrictions on deceptive practices, its advocates generally find an implied claim that the product delivers a considerably broader environmental benefit than the ad's specific claim.

---

[31]Ultimately, the externality problem described in the previous paragraph may mean that so few consumers will demand environmentally improved products that such products will not be produced. If so, and if the costs of government regulation are less than the costs of the externality, then a governmental solution would be appropriate. If regulatory solutions are appropriate, however, the regulators should justify those regulations directly, rather than under the guise of how advertising claims should be interpreted.

Another approach to regulating environmental claims is possible and preferable. The traditional FTC approach to advertising regulation makes no attempt to divine ideal environmental policy. Rather, it examines the offer made to consumers, and it asks whether the product performs as promised. Claims are permitted if the manufacturer has a reasonable basis to conclude that the product indeed possesses the claimed feature. Under the advertising policy approach to degradability claims, for example, the issue is whether the product degrades, not whether degradability is less preferable than recyclability or has other environmental flaws.

The fundamental advantage of the advertising policy approach is its respect for consumer sovereignty. Of course, environmental claims convey a message of some environmental benefit to consumers. Sound regulation should seek to ensure that consumers receive the benefit for which they bargained, even when the claim is phrased in general terms. But sound regulation should not adopt the notion that a claim of a specific benefit implies a general claim that the effect is important to the environment in all circumstances. Sound regulation should require that a product claiming it is compostable must degrade in composting facilities. It should not require the advertiser to disclose the significance of the lack of compostability as an environmental problem, nor should it attempt to evaluate the appropriate role of compostability in the management of solid wastes. Consumer choices should guide market decisions rather than the regulator's views of the choices consumers should make.

Proponents of the regulatory approach might object that the externality problem discussed above justifies their position. The externality problem, however, argues for a different regulatory approach, aimed at correcting the externality itself. Indeed, economists have long advocated that environmental regulation should change incentives to ensure that market choices reflect the full social costs they impose.[32] The solution could be, for example, to raise the price of trash collection to make consumers face the full price of disposal, not to engage in strained interpretations of advertising. Even if the presence of externalities justifies direct regulation of the environmen-

---

[32]See, for example, Robert W. Hahn, "Economic Prescriptions for Environmental Problems: How the Patient Followed the Doctor's Orders," *Journal of Economic Perspectives*, vol. 3 (1989), p. 95.

tal characteristics of products, it hardly argues for manipulating the information available to consumers. Furthermore, proponents of the regulatory approach have shown that they are hardly omniscient regarding which policy to follow, as the degradable plastic saga illustrates. After requiring degradability in plastic bags, some states attacked manufacturers for so labeling their products, because they decided that degradability was an ineffective solution for the disposal problem.

If consumers pay the full cost for their decision, informed participants will continue to make a particular choice only if the benefits are worth the costs. There is no such assurance when regulators restrict the flow of information. Indeed, to the extent that market outcomes under the environmental regulation approach differ from the results under the advertising policy approach, it is because consumers are kept ignorant of alternatives they would prefer. When the law allows firms to inform consumers, competition among producers for the dollars of environmentally conscious consumers will remove any need to design advertising rules that attempt to control the flow of information to consumers.

As reflected in the *Green Report II*, state attorneys general are firmly in the camp of the environmental regulators. Although the report acknowledges the role of the market, it is viewed as "a powerful tool that can be used" to achieve environmental objectives.[33] Numerous recommendations reflect explicit or implicit judgments about the ideal environmental policy and structure the recommended marketing claims to achieve that objective. Indeed the tone of the report is set early, when the task force maintains that such general claims as being "environmentally friendly" or "safe for the environment" should be avoided, because "the production and use of products necessarily have adverse environmental consequences."[34]

No example of the states' viewpoint is clearer than the report's treatment of "trivial and irrelevant" claims. The report cautions that such claims should be avoided, and offers the following example:

> An example of a technically accurate but irrelevant claim
> is a polystyrene foam cup that claims to "preserve our trees

---

[33]*Green Report II*, p. v. The acknowledgment of the market's role was not present in the original *Green Report*.

[34]Ibid., p. 5.

and forests." It is simply irrelevant, and perhaps deceptive, to suggest that a product made of petroleum products, a scarce, nonrenewable natural resource, provides an environmental benefit because it does not use trees, the natural renewable resource that would have been used if the cup had been made of paper instead of polystyrene.[35]

Some states used this provision to win packaging changes from Dart Industries, which had noted on packaging for its foam cups that they "preserve our trees and forests."[36] Although both forest and petroleum resources are scarce, these states apparently believe that consumers should not be given information to facilitate their choice. Or perhaps they believe that consumers should prefer renewable materials over non-renewable ones. Yet if consumers prefer to save forests rather than fossils, it is not apparent why advertising regulators should care.

Similarly, the report expresses concerns about third-party seals of approval for environmental attributes. It notes that

the ongoing public debate about the relative merits of paper and plastic bags might tempt a program to award seals in a "grocery bag" category. However, experts agree that, whenever possible, shoppers should avoid disposable bags and carry their own reusable bags.[37]

Presumably the same rationale would apply to comparative claims by paper or plastic bag makers, that their product is better for the environment. By this view, truth is irrelevant. Instead, to promote the choice the regulator believes desirable, information is suppressed concerning the issue most consumers confront regularly—should we ask for paper or plastic?

Beyond simple respect for the choices consumers make, there are sound reasons for the advertising policy approach. First, it avoids the need to resolve difficult scientific issues, especially in a field in which the science is changing rapidly. Even if one could resolve such issues, the conclusions would run the risk of rapid obsolescence.[38]

---

[35]Ibid., p. 28.

[36]See Jerry Taylor, "Bossy States Censor Green Ads," *Wall Street Journal*, August 8, 1991.

[37]*Green Report II*, p. 14.

[38]In this context, it is worth noting that McDonald's originally introduced foamed

The difficulties and inevitable delays in altering or revising regulatory standards mandate a flexible approach to the scientific issues. The reasonable-basis doctrine incorporates just such an approach, allowing an assessment of the scientific evidence on a case-by-case basis.

The *Green Report II* reveals the difficulties in requiring resolution of scientific issues. An emerging approach to assessing environmental costs and benefits is the product life-cycle evaluation, in which all beneficial and adverse environmental effects of producing a product are assessed, from obtaining raw materials to manufacturing and ultimately to disposal of the product and manufacturing byproducts.[39] Although the attorneys general recognize that life-cycle assessments "are expected to be extremely useful for evaluating the overall environmental effects of various manufacturing processes and products,"[40] they would prohibit marketing claims based on such assessments:

> The results of product-life assessments should not be used to advertise or promote specific products until uniform methods for conducting such assessments are developed and a general consensus is reached among government, business, environmental, and consumer groups on how this type of environmental comparison can be advertised non-deceptively.[41]

In short, until the scientific issues are definitively resolved, consumers are not to be trusted with the information. As with the FTC's policy toward tar and nicotine measures of cigarettes before 1967,

---

plastic containers because of concern that trees should not be sacrificed to preserve Big Macs. See Scott Hume, "McDonald's Case Study," *Advertising Age* (January 29, 1991), p. 32.

[39]The difficulties that attend life cycle assessments are a potent illustration of Friedrich A. Hayek's observation that competitive markets synthesize and reveal information in ways that are virtually impossible for a central planner. See Friedrich A. Hayek, "The Use of Knowledge in Society," *American Economic Review*, vol. 35 (1945), p. 526. After all, each product's price is a cradle-to-grave life cycle assessment of all of the resources used in its production. The only reason that separate environmental life cycle assessments are needed is that current environmental policy focuses far more on imposing solutions than on identifying and imposing the real costs of various activities on the parties generating those costs.

[40]*Green Report II*, p. 11.

[41]Ibid.

such a policy is likely to impose significant costs on consumers.

This difficulty is inherent in the environmental-regulation approach to marketing claims. Without resolving the scientific issues, one cannot decide which environmental policy to pursue; without a decision about policy, one cannot make choices about which claims to permit or prohibit. Basing the regulatory decision on advertising policy avoids the need to answer such questions. Instead, it reduces the inquiry to the more manageable one of whether a particular piece of research provides a reasonable basis for a particular claim.

The second advantage of the advertising policy approach is the critical importance of context in determining meaning. Most words in common usage do not have one single meaning; instead, meaning depends on context.[42] Regulatory definitions necessarily apply in all contexts, thus ignoring a critical determinant of meaning. In contrast, advertising policy can be used to give concrete guidance about how the context affects the likely interpretation that consumers will attach to various environmental claims.

State policy, as reflected in the *Green Reports*, is somewhat schizophrenic about the significance of context. In recommending federal action, the task force specifically endorses the definitional approach. It argues that

> uniform definitions are needed for terms such as "degradable," "compostable," "recycled," and "recyclable," to assure that marketers know what properties their products must possess before they can make these claims. . . . The federal regulatory program also must include testing protocols and standards for industry to follow in determining whether a product satisfies a particular environmental definition.[43]

This advice, if followed, would necessarily lead to a "one-word, one-meaning" regulatory standard.[44]

---

[42]Thus, the meaning of a sentence like "the heavy light gave just as much light as the light one" is at least reasonably clear, although a nightmare for the regulator who must determine a single definition for "light."

[43]*Green Report II*, p. 1.

[44]Although the recommended federal approach is the same, the initial *Green Report* was considerably more elaborate in its discussion of the need for standardized definitions. See the *Green Report*, pp. 20–27.

On the other hand, the task force's "Recommendations to Industry" are much more sensitive to the importance of context. Particular recommendations are often based on assumptions—not necessarily reasonable ones, as we discuss below—about how consumers are likely to interpret claims. Implicitly they leave open the possibility that different contexts would alter meanings. Frequently the advice given is to provide more, often excessive information, again acknowledging that the meaning of a claim will change with the added disclosure. As presented in the original *Green Report*, however, these "Recommendations to Industry" are transitional in nature. That is, the states' desired outcome is to have uniform, specific definitions, and context is considered a transitional problem.[45]

Of course, the meaning of particular terms employed in environmental advertising is ultimately an empirical question. As the next section demonstrates, we can identify a reasonable interpretation of common claims based on judgments about likely consumer interpretation. Nevertheless, such judgments should be confirmed with consumer surveys. Unfortunately, definitive surveys that would resolve disputes about meaning have not yet been conducted. We discuss the available evidence in the context of particular claims.

At the federal level, proposed legislation is firmly in the environmental regulation camp. The National Waste Reduction, Recycling, and Management Act, H.R. 3865, would set specific standards before manufacturers can use ten environmental terms. Firms could not say "recycled" or "recycled content" unless the product contained at least 25 percent post-consumer materials on the effective date of the regulation, and not less than 50 percent after January 1, 2000. "Recyclable" would be banned unless at least 25 percent of such products are recycled annually nationwide on the effective date of the regulations, and at least 50 percent are annually recycled after 2000. Similarly, "reusable," "refillable," "combustible," "degradable," and similar terms are given specific definitions.[46]

---

[45]*Green Report*, pp. 30–31. The *Green Report II*, p. viii, also offers its recommendation to the business community to ensure compliance with state laws "until concrete and specific federal definitions and standards are in place."

[46]Use of the terms "reusable" and "refillable" requires that the product can be reused an average of five times or more. Use of "combustible" or "degradable"

Although the bill would preempt any inconsistent state law, its distance from the advertising policy approach is revealed by the minimal role given to the FTC. The bill states that the EPA administrator may "promulgate such additional regulation or revise existing regulation as the administrator deems to be necessary to carry out" the bill. The EPA is to have the central role in drafting regulations. A fifteen-member Independent Advisory Board on Environmental Marketing Claims is established to advise the EPA. The FTC has one, nonvoting member on the board. Once the board reports, it will be terminated within sixty days, after which the EPA will consult with the FTC merely "as necessary and appropriate." Once the EPA adopts a regulation, the FTC's only role will be to enforce it. The FTC could not use its advertising policy approach.

Particular Environmental Claims

Recycled Content Claims. Claims concerning recycled materials raise two fundamental issues: how much recycled material is necessary before the claim is allowed? and what materials are recycled? The states maintain that claims of recycled content should be accompanied by separate disclosures of the percentage of material that is preconsumer waste or postconsumer waste.[47]

Pre- versus post-consumer waste. Like the proposed federal legislation discussed above, the state task force argues that material is only "recycled" if it is postconsumer waste, meaning that a consumer actually used it. The states claim is as follows:

> Realistically, when consumers think about recycling, they are thinking only about post-consumer waste—the trash they leave at the curb. The Task Force is of the opinion that consumers commonly believe that products labeled "recycled" contain material that consumers have recycled, *i.e.*, household waste, that has been separated out by the

---

requires that 25 percent of the products are "managed annually in a waste management system that is protective of human health and the environment" on the regulation's effective date and that at least 50 percent are so managed in the next century.

[47]*Green Report II*, p. 8.

consumer for separate collection by a recycler and used in creating new products.[48]

This view of consumer expectations confuses the consumers' role as demanders of recycled material with their role as suppliers of material for recycling. Because consumers supply only postconsumer material, the states assume that they demand only postconsumer material as well. But there is little basis and no empirical evidence to support such an assumption.

Indeed, the available evidence indicates that consumers do not distinguish between pre- and postconsumer waste. Asked about the meaning of the term "recycled," virtually no consumers indicate that the source of the waste matters to them. The most commonly offered answers were, "Made from previously used materials/waste" (49.8 percent of responses) or "made from recycled materials" (23.7 percent). When asked what word they would use to describe packaging made from manufacturing scraps or collected from community recycling centers, a nearly identical number chose "recycled" in both cases (33 percent of preconsumer waste, 38 percent for postconsumer). This in fact was the only description chosen ahead of "don't know" in both cases. Asked what "made from preconsumer or postconsumer waste" means, two-thirds to three-quarters of consumers did not know. Of those who did know, the predominant answer was "recycled."[49]

A more reasonable view of the expectations of consumers as demanders of recycled products is that they are seeking to reduce the solid-waste problem.[50] If so, any material that would otherwise have been trash is appropriately labeled as "recycled." The relevant question is thus whether the material would have been trash but for the recycling.

---

[48]*Green Report II*, p. 9.

[49]Brenda J. Cude, *Comments Prepared for the November 1991 EPA Public Hearings on Use of the Terms Recycled and Recyclable and the Recycling Emblem in Environmental Marketing Claims*, tables 1, 6–9, pp. 17, 22–25. The results are based on combining a series of surveys conducted through the University of Illinois Cooperative Extension Service. Because different surveys asked different questions, sample sizes varied from 199 to 645 respondents on invidivual questions.

[50]One might also argue that consumers demand recycled materials to reduce consumption of natural resources. Again, however, the source of the recycled material is irrelevant.

This test focuses on materials that are diverted from the waste stream, at the cost of some additional effort. Materials are not recycled, however, when they can be recombined with virgin material with only trivial additional steps.[51] Thus virgin material does not become recycled if the manufacturer drops it on the floor and then picks it up. It is very unlikely that such material would otherwise become trash. Conversely, paper scraps that result from cutting envelopes to the proper shape may well become trash, without some significant additional steps to reuse the material.[52]

In the absence of definitive evidence about consumer expectations, the principle of regulatory caution argues for making no distinction between pre- and postconsumer wastes. If consumers do care about material that is recycled from consumer sources, some manufacturers may claim that their products incorporate "post consumer material." If such claims are made, then clearly regulators should protect them. Claims that postconsumer material is used would be deceptive unless they were true, because the manufacturer has specified a particular source of material. Advertising regulators can protect affirmative representations, however, without treating the more general claim of being "recycled" in a way that is more specific than its common usage. Without strong evidence that it matters to consumers, there is no reason to create an artificial distinction that advertisers must explain away.[53]

---

[51]One should also distinguish between joint products and material that would otherwise become trash. Cows, for example, yield leather as a joint product of meat production. Obviously, such products are not recycled.

[52]The "otherwise trash" test is, we admit, somewhat imprecise. There is no bright-line distinction between trivial and significant steps that may be necessary to divert a particular material from the waste stream. Particularly when the question concerns the reasonableness of thinking the material would otherwise have been trash, however—as it does under the FTC's substantiation doctrine—these ambiguities hardly seem insurmountable.

[53]An example of creating irrelevant distinctions is that of the old FTC in dealing with rerefined or recycled oil. Because it believed that consumers preferred "new" oil, the commission required sellers of recycled oil to identify their product as "re-refined." Mohawk Ref. Co., 54 FTC 1071 (1958), 263 F.2d 818 (3rd Cir. 1959). Because the evidence showed that rerefined oil was as satisfactory as oil made from virgin crude, the result was to create an artificial barrier to recycling. The minimal market for recycled oil led the commission to suspend partially its Trade Regulation Rule requiring disclosure of the prior use of oil in 1981. *Federal Register*, vol. 46 (April 8, 1981), p. 20,979.

Although partially cloaked in the language of consumer beliefs, the regulatory basis for the states' position is quite explicit:

> Because solid-waste managers are often unable to locate markets for materials that consumer discard, state policy makers have sought to stimulate these markets by requiring that specific amounts of postconsumer material be incorporated into products before they can be labeled as "recycled."[54]

Even as environmental policy, however, the states' approach is flawed. It creates artificial distinctions that could significantly complicate the market for recycled materials. Unless regulators create one, there is no reason for recyclers to track the sources of their material and identify the quantities from each source. Imposing such a requirement could have perverse effects: it could lead a recycler to reject certain types of waste, to ensure that all his material came from a certain source. Certainly, it would raise the costs of handling and using recycled materials, whether pre- or postconsumer, and this effect could only reduce the use of recycling.

More fundamentally, the states' position could well lead to an increase in the amount of solid waste. To the extent that consumer demand for recycled products is an important reason for recycling—and the states' position assumes that it is—that demand can be met from lower-cost industrial waste or higher-cost consumer waste.[55] The effect of prohibiting claims that products made with industrial trash are recycled is to eliminate the low-cost source of supply for recycled materials. Thus the cost of recycled material will increase, and the quantity actually used will decline. The result is more trash, not less.[56] Concerns such as these led the EPA to conclude tentatively

---

[54] *Green Report II*, p. 9.

[55] We make the conventional assumption that because it is cleaner, more uniform, and generated in fewer locations, industrial waste is the lower cost source of recycled material.

[56] We assume that consumer demand for the material will be higher if it is called "recycled" than if less familiar terms are used, such as "reprocessed industrial waste." This assumption means that there will be more trash even if industrial waste is a higher-cost source of recycled material. Unless additional material that qualifies for the "recycled" label is available at constant marginal cost, restricting use of the term will increase the amount of trash.

that the definition of recycled material should not distinguish between pre- and postconsumer waste.[57]

Disclosure of recycled content. The states' approach of requiring disclosure of the recycled material content is also flawed, even if it is simplified to a disclosure that does not distinguish between pre- and postconsumer waste (—that is, *x* percent recycled paper). The EPA's preferred option is also to require disclosure of the percentage of recycled material.[58] Disclosure raises the costs of communicating about recycled products.[59] It would be better to treat a claim that a product is recycled as a claim that the product incorporates the maximum amount of recycled material that is technologically feasible without affecting the functional properties of the material, as long as this amount is significant.

The available survey evidence suggests that the fraction of recycled material is relatively unimportant to consumers. Asked about the meaning of "recycled" on a product package, consumers do not volunteer that the amount matters. Asked specifically, "Is it important to you to know if the packaging is all recycled material or some new and some recycled?" only 38 percent said yes. About half—48 percent—said this information was unimportant; an additional 14 percent either did not know or did not answer. In contrast, 63 and 64 percent said they would purchase a product labeled recycled over one that was not, in responses concerning recycled paper towels and recycled plastic shampoo bottles, respectively.

Of those who gave a reason for wanting the information, 20 percent wanted to police firms that claim a product is recycled when it actually contained only trivial amounts—1–10 percent—of recycled material; 15 percent wanted the information to *avoid* recycled products.[60] These findings hardly suggest that claims of recycled

---

[57]*Federal Register*, vol. 56 (1991), p. 49,996. The EPA was seeking comment on the tentative advice that it planned to give to the FTC.

[58]Ibid.

[59]Although this disclosure is relatively inexpensive, the key factor is its costs relative to the claim that makes it necessary. Many environmental claims are likely merely to mention a relevant attribute, rather than to be the primary message of an advertisement or a label. Thus, even short disclosures may increase significantly the relative cost of the environmental claim compared with other information.

[60]Cude, *Environmental Marketing Claims*, table 10 and appendix, p. 43. The

content are deceptive in the absence of a percentage disclosure. Unless the amount of recycled material is trivial, consumers apparently read a "recycled" designation in a binary way—either it is or it is not.

It is difficult to use consumer survey evidence to set a minimum percentage requirement for recycled content, or even to ask whether a product with a particular percentage qualifies as recycled. Sensible answers depend on more information than typical survey respondents are likely to have. Information about the technological constraints and about how a given percentage of recycled content compares with the technological frontier is likely to be relevant to both consumer and expert assessments of whether the product is recycled. A straightforward question about how much material should qualify a product as recycled will reflect not only consumers' estimates of how much is needed, but also their assessment of where the technological frontier may lie. The relevant question is, given a technological frontier for a particular product of 15 percent, would consumers consider a product with 15 percent recycled content as recycled?

Although consumer expectations should provide the baseline for regulation of advertising claims, it is neither possible nor desirable to develop definitions consistent with every consumer perception that a claim may convey. Regulators must recognize that some or even most consumers will be confused, particularly in the early stages of providing information about a new product attribute. Redefining words because some consumers misuse them, however, is unlikely to facilitate the process of conveying information. According to 10 percent of consumers, for example, a "recycled" plastic shampoo bottle has been used before or is refillable.[61] But even a significant greater confusion would not warrant writing the distinction between recycled and reusable products out of marketers' language.

In the absence of consumer surveys that specifically address the question, the issue is hardly free from doubt. But the technological approach is consistent with likely consumer interpretations of the term "recycled." Indeed, of those consumers who gave a reason for

---

sample size for these questions was 199. Twenty-four percent of consumers with a reason and 7 percent of all consumers wanted information because a higher proportion of recycled material is important.

[61]Ibid., table 3; 6.7 percent thought the bottle had been used before, 3.4 percent thought it could be reused, and 0.4 percent thought it was refillable.

not wanting information about the recycled fraction, 26 percent said it was because they assumed that a "recycled" label implied the recycling of as much material as practically possible.[62] Products such as corrugated cardboard boxes, long thought of and labeled as recycled, incorporate substantial amounts of virgin materials because of technological constraints.[63] Such linguistic usage predates the current emphasis on environmental attributes. Furthermore, the technological approach preserves the maximum possible incentives to use recycled materials. Even when the maximum feasible amount of recycled material is 15 percent, for example, consumers may believe that a product claiming 15 percent recycled-material content is not extensively recycled. Such an interpretation would be errone-ous, but it could well deter recycled-material claims and the use of recycled material. And of those interested in the percentage recy-cled, many want the information to determine whether the amount of recycled content is trivial.

When the only constraints concern such issues as the product's appearance, these considerations are less relevant.[64] A product with as little as 15 percent or as much as 75 percent of recycled content is not making extensive use of recycled material in such cases, given the possibilities. Here disclosure of the actual amount of recycled material is appropriate. Without disclosure, the claim may convey more recycled material than is actually the case.[65]

If disclosures are required, of course, manufacturers of products with low recycled content who are at the technological frontier could try to explain that 15 percent recycled content, for example, was the

---

[62]Ibid., p. 42, appendix. This result is 4.5 percent of the entire sample (1991). Although small, the answer was volunteered to an unprompted question. Moreover, *no* consumers volunteered that they thought a recycled product was 100 percent recycled.

[63]In discussions with grocery product manufacturers, we were told that recycled corrugated boxes contain a maximum of about 17 percent recycled material. The constraints are likely to differ for different materials and are likely to change over time as technology improves.

[64]Recycled paper, for example, may not be as white or as uniform in color as paper from virgin material.

[65]For similar reasons, we would not allow a product to say "recycled," even though it is at the technological frontier, when the amount of recycled material is trivial. In such cases, percentage disclosure is appropriate—for example, "3 percent recycled"—to avoid misleading consumers.

103

maximum practical amount. That information, however, might be difficult to convey. At the very least, the need to explain it increases the cost of a disclosure requirement. In the absence of strong evidence that the percentage of recycled material is important to consumers (as long as the amount is not trivial), a better solution is to let the market reveal whether consumers value the information by letting firms provide the information if it is useful. Requiring the information unnecessarily simply creates the need to explain away an artificial distinction.

One effect of the technological-feasibility approach is that a product with only 20 percent recycled material might claim it is "recycled" while another product that does not reach the technological limits can claim only "30 percent recycled content." Consumers might prefer the product with a higher recycled-material content but would not be able to identify it. Although the states' requirement for all products to disclose their recycled-material content would avoid this problem, it creates problems of its own.

Environmental choices are necessarily multidimensional, and there is no reason to reserve the term "recycled" for the ideal product. There is no basis to presume that the product with the higher recycled-material content is preferable, without a detailed reckoning of environmental benefits and costs. To reduce solid waste, for example, what matters most is presumably the *volume* of material diverted from landfills, which may be differently related to the percentage of recycled material by *weight* across different materials.[66] Short of tracking the source of all trash in enormous detail, however, there is little likelihood of reliable measurements based on volume. Moreover, significant competition is likely to occur between different products of the same general type, rather than among different materials.[67]

Finally, as noted above, the percentage-disclosure approach may itself mislead consumers about the extent of recycling that is occurring when the limitations are technological but the percentage

---

[66]Although the *Green Report II* would require disclosure, it does not specify how the disclosure would be calculated. The EPA would calculate the percentage based on weight. *Federal Register*, vol. 56 (1991), p. 49,997.

[67]The elasticity of substitution, for example, between competing cardboard packaging materials is likely to be higher than the elasticity of substitution between cardboard and plastic packaging.

of recycled material is relatively low. Consumers may regard "20 percent recycled" as not sufficiently recycled, even when they would prefer a recycled container if they knew 20 percent was the best that could be done. For these reasons, it seems preferable and more consistent with consumer expectations to treat the "recycled" claim as meaning that the product is as recycled as currently possible.

Recyclable, Degradable, or Compostable. Determinations about regulation should recognize that claims of being "recyclable" or "compostable" are claims about ability, not likelihood. Consumers presumably understand, for example, that a "washable" suit is one capable of being washed, not one that will be washed; that "perishable" means a product will deteriorate under certain conditions; and that "flammable" means the product can burn, not that a fire is likely. Thus regulators should treat a claim of recyclability as a claim that the product can be recycled, not a claim about the likelihood that recycling will occur.[68]

The states, however, would treat such claims as implying that recycling facilities exist. In its initial report, the task force took the position that this claim is location-specific—that is, in each area where the claim is made, recycling facilities must exist.[69] The task force's final report allows unqualified claims only for "nationally sold products that are generally recyclable everywhere."[70] The report recognizes that aluminum cans can claim they are "recyclable" without qualification.[71]

If a product is recycled "in many areas," the states would permit a "qualified recyclability claim." The precise nature of the necessary qualifications is unclear. The task force "strongly recommends" that companies set up 800-numbers to provide consumers with the loca-

---

[68]Our discussion focuses on claims of recyclability, but the same principles are applicable to other "-able" claims as well.

[69]*Green Report*, pp. 38–42. This position applies as well to claims about compostability. Some states have adopted similar restrictions by statute. California, for example, requires that each county with a population above 300,000 must have recycling facilities before a recyclable claim can be made statewide. 1990 Cal. Stats. Ch. 1443. This statute is constitutionally dubious, as we discuss below.

[70]*Green Report II*, p. 21.

[71]See also the *Green Report II*, p. 25; recyclable claims are permitted only if "a significant amount of the product is being recycled everywhere the product is sold."

tion of the nearest recycling facility. The only example of a permissible claim offered is the following:

> Recyclable in many communities. Call us at (800) xxx-xxxx to find out if there is a recycling facility that accepts this product near you. Support recycling. [72]

The difficulties of including this mouthful in television advertising are obvious. It remains to be determined whether the more limited claim that the product is "recyclable in many communities" is acceptable.

If a company wishes to make a capability claim for a product that is not recycled "in many areas," the states' position amounts to a virtual prohibition:

> That company should clearly disclose all of the material facts, including at least: (1) the fact that the technology is in the early stages, or that there are only "pilot" recycling programs, if that is the case; (2) the number of locations where the product is being recycled; (3) the types of collection sites if there is no curbside pick-up available (e.g. "at school cafeterias"); and (4) the number of states in which the collection and recycling facilities are located. [73]

The EPA is also concerned that recyclable claims imply local availability of recycling facilities, but it would approach the problem in a slightly different fashion. Its provisionally preferred option is to allow recyclable claims if they do not imply that the product is recyclable everywhere, if they provide information that would assist consumers in recycling the material, and if they disclose the national recycling rate of the product or material. A glass bottle could for example claim "this bottle is recyclable in communities where collection facilities for colored glass bottles exist. For more informa-

---

[72]Ibid., p. 25.

[73]Ibid., p. 26. It is of interest to note that this limitation on claiming recyclability conflicts with the requirements of other states that items be clearly marked as recyclable. Thus, for example, in North Carolina, only recyclable plastic bags are allowed to be carried by retailers. Notice of recyclability "shall" be printed on each bag, and until 1993 the availability of recycling facilities is irrelevant to the printing of the required notification of "recyclable." See N.C. States Ch. 130A Public Health section 309.10.

tion contact your local recycling coordinator. Glass bottles are recycled at a 20 percent rate nationally."[74] Although they are more sensitive to the need to provide information about recyclability in circumstances where facilities are not widely available, the extensive disclosure requirements would still pose considerable difficulties, particularly in broadcast advertising. Furthermore, the utility of the national recycling rate for consumer decisions is dubious at best. It reflects both the availability of facilities and the extent to which consumers are willing to use them. Thus it is difficult to view the measure as a proxy for the likelihood that facilities exist within easy reach of a particular consumer.

The available survey evidence offers little indication that consumers infer from a claim of recyclability that local facilities exist. Asked about the meaning of "recyclable" on a plastic shampoo bottle, two-thirds of consumers understood the term to mean that the bottle could be recycled. Just over half gave that answer for a glass jar, where nearly one-third thought "recyclable" meant the jar could be reused.[75] Although they were not asked directly about availability of local facilities, availability was not significant enough for consumers to mention on their own.

Of course, virtually any product can be recycled if someone is willing to devote unlimited time and effort to the task. Interpreting recyclability as a claim that recycling is possible given unlimited resources would therefore deprive the word of all meaning. Thus, distinguishing between the conceptual possibility of recycling and the actual ability to do so is essential. Claims without qualification that a product is "recyclable" should be permitted either if collection points are widely available or if they are likely to be so in the near future.

Both consumer interpretation and general policy considerations argue for interpreting recyclability claims as meaning that a product

---

[74]*Federal Register*, vol. 56 (1991), p. 49,997.

[75]Cude, *Environmental Marketing Claims*, p. 12. The sample size for these questions was 233. As noted above, there is no reason to protect the incorrect expectation of a third of consumers that a recyclable glass jar is in fact reusable. That is particularly true since a majority of consumers understand the term correctly. Moreover, it is not apparent how consumers might choose differently if the distinction were explained, thus undercutting the rationale for any required disclosure that "recyclable products are not reusable."

can be recycled. Consumers interested in recycling surely understand that most recycling requires effort on their part.[76] It is not reasonable to conclude that consumers expect someone to sort their garbage. For a consumer who purchases a recyclable product but does not recycle it, the existence of recycling facilities is irrelevant. Currently, a consumer who wishes to recycle the product must undertake the effort to locate the facility, determine its procedures, and collect and deliver the material appropriately sorted.[77] Obviously the likelihood of recycling depends on what the consumer does, not on what the manufacturer says about the product.

Nonetheless, the manufacturer's ability to provide truthful information about recyclability is important. Recycling depends on the presence of both recycling facilities and recyclable products. If only because of the difficulties of coordination, the two are unlikely to emerge simultaneously. Unless consumers can readily identify recyclable materials, there is little incentive to establish programs and facilities to collect those materials. For a new material or a newly recyclable use of an existing material, there is no reason to establish recycling facilities until it is clear that consumers will purchase the product. Except for recyclable products that are obviously identifiable and widely used, such as newspapers or aluminum cans, claims of recyclability are likely to precede the widespread emergence of recycling facilities. There is no reason to make the necessary investments until the product is in the hands of consumers interested in recycling.

The states' approach—requiring disclosure of limited availability when facilities are not available everywhere—has a superficial appeal. In fact, however, it will cause problems. When facilities are widely available but are unavailable in a few places, such a disclaimer serves no useful purpose for consumers. Requiring a dis-

---

[76]Thus, when asked whether they would purchase a product labeled recyclable, some consumers volunteer that they would not do so because local facilities are not available. Cude, *Environmental Marketing Claims*, tables 14 and 15.

[77]It is possible that claims of recyclability may lead consumers to place products in recycling collection bins that contaminate the stream of material, thereby raising cost. Even detailed "where facilities exist" disclosures, however, would not solve this problem. The problem is that "facilities" exist, but consumers use them inappropriately.

108

claimer when facilities are available may actually complicate the problem facing consumers trying to determine whether recycling facilities exist in a particular area. If virtually all products must limit the claim to areas "where facilities exist," then consumers cannot distinguish the product for which facilities are widely available from a competing product, for which they are limited.

The limiting language that a product is recyclable "where facilities exist" can serve a useful purpose for both consumers and advertisers. It can allow identification of products that are in fact recyclable but for which facilities are not widespread and evidence on future availability does not exist. Such claims are likely to be appropriate in the early stages of recycling programs for many materials. The phrase, however, is not a talisman. It should convey the information that recycling is available in a reasonable number of locations, but not widely. Indiscriminate use destroys its ability to do so.

Moreover, because the claim that a product is "recyclable" is a claim about capability rather than likelihood or actuality, such claims should be permissible in some instances even when facilities are not widely available. As discussed above, actual recycling requires both collection points and the consumer's ability to identify recyclable products for separation and collection. Claims of recyclability are likely to precede wide availability of facilities, because little incentive exists to develop facilities in the absence of information in the hands of consumers. If a manufacturer can demonstrate the likelihood of widespread availability of collection points in the future by showing that facilities are under construction or that such facilities would be profitable, the claim of recyclability is not deceptive.

As a practical matter, claims of recyclability based on predictions of future availability are likely to be rare. Obviously, any prediction of future availability is subject to dispute. Thus most advertisers are likely to make the more limited claim, that a product is "recyclable where facilities exist." Nonetheless, proof of future availability should be sufficient to substantiate the claim.

The attitude of some states toward recyclability claims raises another issue—the applicability of the First Amendment. In California, for example, the following claim, actually made by a firm, is illegal:

109

The body of this can is steel. This material is recyclable where steel recycling facilities exist. Support recycling in your community.[78]

This claim is true. Under the constitutional decisions protecting commercial speech discussed above, it is difficult to justify a blanket prohibition on truthful claims.

General Environmental Claims. Determining the meaning of general claims of "environmental safety" or "environmental friendliness" is difficult. They may well be puffery, conveying no specific claims at all. Conversely, such claims might convey specific environmental benefits. In the states' view, they are claims of environmental perfection. "The production and use of products necessarily have adverse environmental consequences . . . ," according to the *Green Report II*, and so "these claims should be avoided altogether. . . . Instead, claims should be specific and state the precise environmental benefit that the product provides."[79]

Because of the difficulty of generalizing about the meaning of safety-and-friendliness claims, it is hard to offer much beyond the advice to make more specific claims. When an advertiser provides a specific meaning, however, such as "environmentally friendly because it is recyclable," there is no reason to assume he has made any additional claim by the use of the term environmentally friendly. Because the context identifies the reason for the product's friendliness, the claim should not be interpreted as implying any more general kind of benefit.

An alternative approach would be to declare that general claims of environmental safety and friendliness are mere puffery, and therefore not subject to regulation. Even if consumers assign some meaning to such claims, this approach is likely to devalue it rapidly. This nonregulatory approach carries some merit, but the claims may well have meaning. In the absence of hard evidence, it seems preferable to encourage clarification. But regulators should not discourage the use of general terms that could enhance the effectiveness

---

[78]Association of National Advertisers, et al. v. Lungren, complaint, p. 22 (N.D. Cap. 2-5-92).

[79]*Green Report II*, p. 5.

or memorability of a communication when the context gives a more specific meaning.

Environmental Marketing—Conclusion

Like health claims, environmental advertising can be regulated by advertising policy, to fulfill consumer expectations and rely on consumer preferences as revealed through the market, or through regulatory policy, to control consumer choices. Perhaps because they seek to avoid the problems that arose with health claims, most participants in the environmental-claims debate are calling upon the Federal Trade Commission to promulgate guidelines.

In the absence of guidelines, many marketers are abandoning efforts to provide consumers with information about environmental attributes. Indeed, one report maintains that "environmental advertising claims are becoming an endangered species."[80] Numerous companies are dropping claims that a product is recycled or recyclable, because of the risk of violating inconsistent state laws.[81] Some companies remain willing to provide environmental information, but only when it is unlikely to be controversial. Others decline to discuss environmental issues in marketing material at all.[82] In other areas, however, particularly ones that the *Green Reports* did not address, companies are exploring the possibilities for environmental claims. Battery makers, for example, are experimenting with "zero-mercury-added" products, prompted in part by state legislative requirements prohibiting mercury by 1996.[83] One can only hope that the political demand for mercury-free batteries will prove more durable than the previous demand for degradable plastics.

Guidelines based on the environmental advertising approaches outlined in this chapter would be useful. Whether the states who participated in the *Green Report* would follow such guidelines is

---

[80]Judann Dagnoli, "Green Ads Wilt: NAD Chief," *Advertising Age* (January 6, 1992), p. 4.

[81]Jennifer Lawrence, "Marketers Drop 'Recycled,' " *Advertising Age* (March 9, 1992), p. 1.

[82]Ibid.

[83]Julie Liesse, "Batteries Getting Greener," *Advertising Age* (February 17, 1992), p. 1.

111

another story. If they did not, the inconsistencies of the health-claims saga would follow. Even if they did, problems would still exist, as we detail in the next chapter.

Another difference between environmental and health claims is that the EPA, the federal agency specifically charged with protecting the environment, has no history of addressing environmental claims, as the FDA has with health claims. It is unclear whether the EPA will take a regulatory position similar to that of the states, or whether Congress will intervene, as it did in the health-claims debate. Again, FTC guidelines would be beneficial if they deterred these developments.

Such guidelines would avoid many problems, if they were to be followed by the EPA and the states and were to lead to congressional abstention. We have stated that problems exist, but thus far we have not delineated them nor discussed why there has been such a divergence between state and federal regulation. We turn next to these issues.

PART THREE

Problems of
Multiple Regulations

Thus far we have focused principally on substance—that of advertising regulation in general and of regulation as specifically applied to health and environmental claims. Two reasons justify this focus. First, one cannot understand the problems that arise from multiple regulation without understanding the benefits and costs of various regulatory approaches. Second, and perhaps more important, in the end it is substance that matters. However significant the procedural costs of multiple regulations, to judge their impact one must understand their substance.

The problems that arise from multiple regulators are procedural— compliance with more than one regulator raises costs; and substantive—multiple regulators necessarily influence the content of national advertising, regardless of whether different substantive standards are applied to evaluate the advertising. Chapter 7 details this perhaps surprising conclusion. Chapter 8 addresses another important issue arising from multiple regulation, namely the effects of the different constraints and incentives facing the regulators. State attorneys general and their staffs do not have the same legal and professional constraints as have those at the Federal Trade Commission. The presence of a second federal regulator—the FDA for health claims, the EPA for environmental claims—provides an additional complication and introduces a third set of constraints and incentives. The career paths and the rewards of each regulator differ in ways that can influence their regulatory approaches.

7
The Impact of
Multiple Regulators
on National Advertising

COMPANIES MARKETING products nationwide use national advertising for simple reasons—it is not economically feasible to adapt advertising campaigns to each individual market, and there is no advantage to doing so. The average cost of producing a television commercial has reached approximately $168,000; the cost of producing fifty, or even ten versions of a campaign will frequently be prohibitive.[1] It is cheaper for a company to purchase television coverage through one network than through a host of individual stations, because it can negotiate with one supplier instead of dozens.

Similarly, major print media are nationally distributed. When different editions are available, they follow economic and marketing boundaries rather than the borders of political jurisdictions. Consumers in different states, and particularly in adjacent ones, have much in common, so they seek similar product information. There is no marketing reason to adapt either print or broadcast campaigns to different state jurisdictions.

The problem of state regulation arises from the external effects of the decisions of any regulator. The costs of adapting advertising campaigns to individual jurisdictions are not worth incurring. Indeed, every national advertiser that has reached a settlement with a state challenger has abandoned the claim nationwide.[2] Consequently,

---

[1]"Programing and Business—Side Developments in Broadcasting," *Advertising Age* (August 7, 1989), p. 46. Cost varies considerably for different product categories and for individual commercials. For packaged goods spots, the average cost was $127,000.

[2]This conclusion applies to national advertising, rather than to national advertisers.

individual-state enforcement actions create national advertising policy. Unfortunately, however, the effects of state decisions are asymmetric. A state can permit a particular advertisement, but that permission has no practical significance if another state decides to restrict the same advertisement.

The extraterritorial impact of state enforcement decisions also means that the traditional "laboratory" justification for a federal system does not apply. State decisions do not generate contrasting regulatory environments for academics to study. Moreover, the state official that initiates an enforcement action receives the benefits of doing so, in the form of publicity. If that decision is wrong, however, citizens of other states, who collectively outnumber those in any one state, will bear the major portion of the costs of the error. Moreover, it is difficult for voters to evaluate the effects of their attorney general's policies, even when they take the time to do so. Thus, there is little political pressure on elected state officials to reverse inappropriate decisions.

State regulation of national advertising in effect provides a series of central governments, responsive only to a portion of the population they govern. Similarly, the extraterritorial effect of a state's act means that only a portion of the affected population is represented in the normal checks of legislative oversight and appropriations. Further, because state statutes are at issue, federal judicial oversight is more limited. In the end, when state regulation is effective it becomes a national substitute for regulation from Washington.

The difficulty and cost of adapting national advertising to individual markets argues strongly for a single set of legal rules to govern such advertising. Just as companies use one ad campaign nationwide, they should be able to produce that ad under one set of legal rules. Otherwise the cost of producing national advertising increases considerably. We describe two primary sources of costs. First, we demonstrate how multiple regulators reduce the informational content of advertising even if the same standards are applied. Second, we address the impact of different regulatory standards. We then com-

---

Advertising that is inherently more localized in nature, such as that for a particular type of clothing, can be more easily (although hardly without cost) adapted to particular regulatory jurisdictions. Such a response is not possible, however, for health or environmental claims in national marketing campaigns.

118

bine the impact of multiple regulators, interpretations, and standards to evaluate the different legal regimes that can result.

Problems of Multiple Interpretations

Even if the states and the federal government were in complete agreement on the standards to apply to advertising regulation, the escalating level of state enforcement activity against national campaigns would be likely to reduce the usefulness of advertising to consumers. Applying any general standard is difficult in close cases. Enforcement necessarily involves an exercise of judgment about which reasonable people can disagree. Advertisers can predict the concerns of an agency with which they have had experience, such as the Federal Trade Commission, and plan their advertising to be consistent with such concerns. It is much more difficult, however, for national advertisers to predict the judgments of numerous state attorneys general. When disagreements arise, the most restrictive judgment will prevail, not the one that most accurately assesses the effect of advertising on consumers. Without a forum to resolve the inevitable differences of opinion among enforcers, the safest course for a national advertiser is to restrict its claims to those that cannot be challenged, thereby reducing the amount of information available to consumers.

The problems confronting national advertisers can best be understood by imagining a baseball game with fifty-one, or even five, different umpires. Even though the rules are clear, and often spelled out in excruciating detail, each umpire will call plays as he sees them. When the play is unmistakable, this arrangement poses few problems. But in a close play, if *any one* of the umpires believes a player is out, scoring will plummet. In such a situation, the most restrictive judgment ultimately prevails, even if the vast majority of umpires reaches the opposite conclusion. As a result, the game is less, not more, likely to be scored according to the general view of the rules.

One might object that caution is warranted in evaluating claims regarding topics such as health. To extend the baseball metaphor, perhaps the fewer runs the better. But this view fails to recognize the costs of the different mistakes that regulators can make. As we discussed above, consumers can mistakenly fail to rely on a true

119

claim or they can mistakenly rely on a false claim.[3] For claims about the relationship between diet and disease, the consequences are relatively small and primarily economic for mistakenly approving a claim that subsequent research might disprove. Banning the ones that later research proves to be true would slow the realization of significant public health benefits. Without a significant risk to consumers from a claim that significant evidence provisionally supports, the government should take care to avoid prohibiting the claim. Fewer runs turn out to harm consumers, not help them.

In the environmental area, the issues are less likely to turn on complex questions of proof. So far, at least, they have involved the broader implications of claims that are accurate in particular circumstances. Excessive caution in developing or applying a regulatory standard sacrifices the opportunity to make incremental environmental progress. Recyclability, for example, is a valuable attribute in areas with appropriate facilities. Restricting such claims on the grounds that facilities are not available everywhere sacrifices the benefits of such claims where they are useful. The claims may not solve problems in areas without facilities, but they do not make problems any worse.[4] Again, fewer runs are more likely to harm consumers than to help them.

More generally, to the extent that caution is warranted, it should be reflected in the substantive standard adopted. With a standard that strikes an appropriate balance between the risks of errors, additional caution in applying the standard is excessive. Just as "conservative" assumptions in risk assessments can combine to produce drastically inflated risk estimates, so excessive caution in applying a standard originally designed to be cautious is likely to produce overly restrictive results.[5] Accordingly, if multiple enforcers are to make independent judgments, their standard should be less restrictive.

In baseball, if we want fewer runs, the appropriate response is to revise the rules. If the rules are good ones, however, the best

---

[3]See chapter 5.

[4]This conclusion is even stronger if allowing claims increases the demand for establishing recycling (or, similarly, composting) facilities, but it does not depend on that possibility.

[5]See *Regulatory Program of the United States Government* (1990), pp. 13–25.

judgment about whether they were followed should prevail, not the most restrictive judgment. The same principle applies to the substantive standards for marketing communications.

Claims about subjective product characteristics such as taste or appearance and advertising that promotes only a product's image pose few risks of differing judgments in applying legal standards. These are the "clear plays" in advertising law, rarely subject to challenge. Claims about novel product characteristics and newly emerging evidence about a product's effects offer more opportunity for differences of opinion, about both the meaning of the advertisement to consumers and the facts upon which the claim is based. If the most restrictive judgment prevails, consumers will lose, as advertisers reduce the risk of challenge by avoiding such claims entirely. Advertisers can compete for market share with appealing imagery and claims about taste, even if competition on important product characteristics would be more useful for consumers. All too often, advertisers will decide that the legal risks of advertising controversial product attributes outweigh the potential profit from providing the information consumers most desire.

The problems of divergent judgments are compounded by the potential difficulties of litigating with the states in contested cases. The threat of lawsuits in different jurisdictions is itself intimidating, and it reduces an advertiser's willingness to contest even groundless state allegations. Some states are well aware of the coercive impact of this threat and have expressed it. A company can face subpoenas, for example, from each of the states "cooperating" in an investigation. The Mobil environmental-claims lawsuit involved several states, using different theories and applying somewhat different state laws and procedures. The risks of multiple lawsuits make it difficult for a company to obtain its day in court even when it is inclined to fight.[6]

Problems of Multiple Standards

The problems of multiple interpretations resulting from state regulation of national advertising are sufficient to warrant serious concern. They are exacerbated by the lack of unanimity among the states, or

---

[6]Although the states themselves are highly reluctant to litigate, they can impose large costs on advertisers other than the costs of litigation. See the next section of this chapter.

121

between the states and the FTC, on the standards that should form the basis for judgments. As the 1989 ABA Report noted, "The FTC's views of appropriate advertising enforcement standards have changed over time, but the views of some state enforcers more closely resemble the FTC's earlier views."[7] Indeed, some states are using standards that those involved with the FTC—both liberals and conservatives, Democrats and Republicans—abandoned well before 1980, and in many instances before 1970.

State use of inappropriate standards creates two problems. First, bad standards yield bad results. When an individual state applies the fools test to prohibit an advertisement that provides valuable information to the vast majority of consumers who interpret the claim correctly, consumers lose. Second, when it is not economically feasible to tailor advertising to individual markets, consumers nationwide can be deprived of the information.

Marketers can sometimes use a simple statement of the limitations of an offer to ensure conformity with conflicting state laws. Many promotional games of chance, for example, are "void where prohibited." No such solution is possible for state regulation of the content of advertising. With different state standards, national advertising must effectively comply with the most restrictive standard found in any state. Thus, differing state standards would lead to "lowest-common-denominator" advertising.

Not all states are alike, of course, and the risk of lowest-common-denominator advertising therefore depends on the states involved. Manufacturers can ignore small states that impose restrictive standards. The general counsel of one company we know informed a small New England state objecting to his company's claims that the company would cease selling its product in that state. Such strategies are not possible for the larger states, however. And three of the largest—California, New York, and Texas—have been among the most aggressive in scrutinizing national advertising.

A second objection to our conclusion is that, to date, the states have not been in the business of enforcing their advertising policy through litigation. Instead they have sought to maximize publicity by challenging advertisements that have stopped, or are about to stop.

---

[7]1989 ABA Report (1989), p. 40, reprinted in *Antitrust and Trade Regulators Report*, vol. 56 (BNA) (Special Supplement, April 6, 1989).

The few firms that chose to fight the states largely succeeded. This objection is true as far as it goes, but it misses the point. Although legally toothless, the states have a weapon that most advertisers appear to fear more: publicity.[8] Economic studies have shown that federal advertising enforcement decreases the stock value of the businesses involved; state enforcement presumably has a similar impact.[9] Indeed, the willingness of most businesses to settle quickly with the states is consistent with that presumption.[10]

The legal toothlessness of much state relief is part of the reason that advertisers are willing to settle rather than fight. Abandoning a single advertising campaign imposes some costs, but unless the challenged claim involved a central feature of the product, the costs are relatively low. Besides, many advertising campaigns have relatively short lives before they are replaced. And assurances of voluntary compliance typically apply only to the challenged claim. Even closely similar claims in the future would be exempt from enforceable santions. Thus, there is little incentive for a company to resist.[11] For consumers, however, the costs in reduced information may be more substantial.

The Resulting Possibilities

We will begin by examining the possibilities in general, and then focus on applying table 7–1 to health claims.

---

[8]Legislation can give a state more enforcement credibility, however, simply by banning product claims that the state attorney general would otherwise have to prove are deceptive. Moreover, the states can impose large legal costs, as the Mobil and May Company cases demonstrate.

[9]See, for example, Sam Peltzman, "The Effects of FTC Advertising Regulation," *Journal of Law and Economics*, vol. 24 (1981), p. 403; Alan D. Mathios and Mark Plummer, "The Regulation of Advertising by the Federal Trade Commission: Capital Market Effects," *Research in Law and Economics*, vol. 12 (1989), p. 77.

[10]At the federal level as well, there are strong incentives to settle and most FTC cases are therefore resolved through consent orders. For many businesses, advertising is a way to produce a favorable public image of a product, and a lengthy proceeding to defend the accuracy of that advertising may generate considerable adverse publicity.

[11]In a few more recent cases, states have entered court injunctions, prohibiting the challenged claims in the future, along with "fencing in" provisions concerning similar claims. Such an approach increases incentives for challenged companies to resist, but to date companies have still found settlement more attractive.

TABLE 7–1
POSSIBLE COMBINATIONS OF SUBSTANTIVE STANDARDS WITH
REGULATORS

Standard	Number of Regulators	
	One	Multiple
Correct	A	B
Incorrect	C	D
Different		E

SOURCE: Authors.

In General. Table 7–1 presents the five possibilities that result from the combination of different standards with one or multiple regulators. The standards applied to regulate advertising can be either correct or incorrect, or in the case of multiple regulators, can be different. Because one regulator would presumably not apply different standards, there are five, not six, possible outcomes. Although the correct and incorrect standards are listed as polar solutions, in practice the difference between them could cover a broad range, as we discuss below.

The ideal regulatory environment for consumers would be a single regulator, enforcing the right standard. This is combination A in the table. Because the standard is correct, substantive costs of inappropriate regulation are minimized. Because there is a single regulator, procedural costs of administering the system are minimized. Adding more enforcers of the standard creates the procedural costs of dealing with multiple regulators. This is the situation represented by combination B.[12] This combination also creates substantive costs, as advertising comes to be governed by the most restrictive judgment about the rules, rather than the most accurate. Combination D, multiple enforcers administering the wrong standard, is worse still. An erroneous initial standard denies valuable informa-

---

[12]We assume that the multiple regulators are in significant jurisdictions, such as Texas, California, and New York. If they are not, they can be ignored, albeit at some cost, as discussed above.

124

THE RESULTING POSSIBILITIES

tion to consumers. The standard is tightened further because it is effectively interpreted according to the most restrictive judgment.[13]

Combination C, one regulator applying the incorrect standard, is preferable to combination D. Although the standard is incorrect, the presence of only one regulator eliminates the costs that arise with the application of the most restrictive judgment.[14] An interesting issue arises regarding whether combination C is preferable to combination B. Clear determinations can be made in the table when comparing combinations A through D horizontally or vertically. One regulator is preferable to more than one, and the correct standard dominates the incorrect one. Such clear-cut conclusions, however, are not possible when comparing combinations B and C, because each solution has one attribute that is preferable. The comparison depends on whether the cost of the incorrect standard, represented in combination C, imposes a greater total cost than that of the multiple regulators, which degrade the application of the correct standard, represented in combination B. The result cannot be known a priori.[15]

The favored business solution for the problem of multiple regu-

---

[13]We conclude, based on the case studies in part two and the other cases we examined in part one, that the states are more restrictive than is optimal. The discussion in the text is therefore based on that assumption. Some states have charged, however, that the FTC was too lenient and that it was the states who applied the correct standard. The following footnotes explore the ranking of the possible outcomes under this assumption.

[14]If the states are correct that the FTC was too lenient, and if state enforcers are too restrictive, it is conceptually possible that multiple regulators are preferable to a single one. The additional stringency resulting from the most restrictive judgment would then be a move in the right direction. The procedural costs of multiple regulators, however, would remain. Moreover, in the case of health and environmental claims, the high cost of overregulation compared with the relatively low cost of underregulating argue strongly that the single regulator would be preferable, even if the standard were too lenient.

[15]If the incorrect standard is too lenient, as the states allege, the comparison remains uncertain. Multiple enforcers of the correct standard would be more restrictive than is optimal, and would also generate additional procedural costs. A single enforcer of an overly lenient standard would impose costs as well. The choice would then depend on the relative costs of overregulating and underregulating, as well as the magnitude of the error from each outcome. Again, in the cases we have examined, the costs of overregulation are more serious.

125

lators has been uniform federal standards with a single federal enforcer, which is achieved in either combination A or C. To obtain such standards, however, some compromise is probably necessary with the advocates of the most restrictive standards, especially because in the absence of preemption, the most restrictive standard is likely to prevail. Thus, the substantive standard that results is too restrictive, as we have seen in the case of health claims. Furthermore, the outcome of the health claims legislation only achieves part of the objective of business—it imposes a uniform standard but retains the possibility of multiple enforcers. Similarly, states have advocated a uniform standard for environmental claims, but they have been explicit about opposing such a standard if it preempts state enforcement.[16]

Even with a single enforcer, however, a uniform but incorrect standard (cell C) may be inferior to multiple enforcers administering the right standard (cell B). A single enforcer minimizes procedural costs, but only by imposing substantive costs that result from the wrong standard. Because they bear the procedural costs directly and, as discussed in the next chapter, may not face the full costs of an inappropriate standard, most businesses prefer the solution of combination C to that of combination B. For consumers, however, the issue is less clear, depending on the particular uniform standard adopted. The combined procedural and substantive costs of multiple enforcement of the right standard may well be lower for consumers than the costs of an incorrect standard uniformly applied; that is, combination B may be better than combination C.

The worst possible solution for consumers seems to be multiple enforcers and multiple standards, as represented in combination E. Each creates problems that greatly hinder the ability of advertising to continue to fulfill its role in a competitive economy. Together, the two problems compound each other. Even with a uniform standard, national advertising will be governed by the most restrictive judgment, because reasonable regulators will differ. Because standards differ, it will be governed by the most restrictive standard. In

---

[16]"It is essential that any federal programs developed to govern environmental marketing claims be enforceable not only by federal regulators, but also by the states. . . . The states would, accordingly, vigorously oppose any statute or regulation that proposes preemption of states' rights in this area." *Green Report II*, p. 2.

combination, the information available to consumers in advertising may be determined by the most restrictive judgment applying the most restrictive standard. It seems hard to imagine a system more likely to discourage advertisers from providing specific product information to consumers. Yet, depending upon the nature of the multiple regulations, combination E could become preferable to combination C or D. To illustrate this point and to provide a more concrete application of the principles revealed in table 7–1, we turn to a detailed application of the table to the health claims debate.

Applying Table 7–1 to Health Claims. For health claims, we have the additional complication of a second federal regulator, the FDA. Although the FDA defers to the FTC regarding advertising, the FDA views advertising as indicating the purpose of the food. If the food is promoted as aiding in disease prevention, the FDA can classify it as a drug. Because drugs cannot be sold without FDA approval, which would require conducting clinical trials, the FDA has in the past successfully prohibited health claims on labels and undoubtedly discouraged such claims in advertising. Furthermore, the FDA was willing to infer disease claims from content claims. Thus it effectively prohibited claims that merely mentioned the lack of saturated fat or cholesterol.

In 1973, the FDA reversed its position on content claims, but it still did not allow reference to specific diseases. Until the 1984 Kellogg campaign promoting the role of dietary fiber in cancer prevention, the FTC regulated the permissible claims under its policies. For cholesterol and saturated-fat content claims, combination A of table 7–1 was the standard, as the FTC applied the appropriate rules.[17] Regarding other health claims, combination C described the situation. Although states could attack both advertising and labeling, regarding national brands they generally refrained from action through 1984.[18]

---

[17]In the various food rule-making proceedings discussed in part one, the FTC considered but ultimately rejected adopting rules that would have severely limited the amount of valuable information presented to consumers.

[18]Perhaps because they were not subject to FDA approval for new products, some food manufacturers resisted FDA policy and in fact advertised their products contrary to FDA rules, even before the early 1970s. See generally Peter Barton Hutt, "Government Regulation of Health Claims in Food Labeling and Advertising,"

The situation changed in 1984, when the National Cancer Institute (NCI) began a campaign to broaden the dissemination of information about the role of dietary fiber in preventing cancer. The NCI cooperated with Kellogg in designing All-Bran labels and ads, and the FTC endorsed the campaign. Although the FDA considered seizing the product as a drug, it ultimately backed down and began to draft regulations to allow some health claims. While the FDA considered its regulations, the FTC evaluated health claims under its flexible reasonable-basis approach. Within a few years, however, some states that were opposed to all health claims entered the regulatory arena and applied standards that severely restricted valuable information.

Even if they had applied the correct standard, the presence of the states would have caused problems. Multiple enforcers applying the FTC's reasonable-basis standard could result in something close to the statutory "significant scientific agreement" standard, because without significant scientific agreement, reasonable enforcers could easily differ about whether the evidence was sufficient to permit the claim. In this scenario, the most restrictive interpretation would prevail. Multiple judgments about the meaning of claims under the advertising-policy standard might well lead to a prohibition on health claims for at least some products with negative nutritional attributes. The scope of the prohibition, however, would probably be less comprehensive than the current statutory one, which requires pre-clearance of the subject matter of claims. Moreover, multiple enforcers of the correct standard would eliminate much of the delay inherent in prohibiting truthful claims until the government can certify them.

Food Drug Cosmetic Law Journal, vol. 41 (1986), p. 3. The FTC regulated such claims pursuant to the policies we have described. Thus, for example, the commission entered orders allowing manufacturers to claim "many doctors recommended" a low-fat, low-cholesterol diet to reduce the risk of heart disease, Standard Brands Inc., 82 FTC 1176 (1973), while also entering an order that permitted egg producers to dispute the relationship between dietary cholesterol and heart disease, provided that they disclosed there was controversy about the issue. National Commission on Egg Nutrition, 88 FTC 89 (1976), affirmed as modified, 570 F.2d 157 (7th Cir. 1977). Thus, for firms defying the FDA, the situation resembled combination E with combination E clearly preferable to combination C. (We say "resemble" because the FDA and the FTC focus primarily, although not exclusively, on different forms of communication.) Because the FTC's position was preferable to the FDA's and because companies were willing to run the risk of FDA action, consumers received more truthful information than they otherwise would have.

Clear disclosure of negative attributes, even if unnecessary, could also have forestalled actions based on theories that the claim implied the product was "perfect." Thus multiple enforcers of the correct standard (combination B) would probably be a better solution than the incorrect statutory standard with a single enforcer (combination C).[19]

Of course, some states were applying the incorrect, not the correct, standard. With the FTC applying the correct standard, the situation was that of combination E. The issue thus arises whether combination E—pre–NLEA—is preferable to combination C or D. As we discussed earlier, this seems to be the worst possible solution for consumers, compounding the costs of multiple enforcers and multiple standards. This conclusion must be qualified, however. If the regulator applying the incorrect standard always evaluates the advertising in question, combination E will quickly become like combination D, and the incorrect standard will dominate. Indeed, the regulator applying the more lenient standards could become irrelevant.

If, as occurred in health claims, the regulators do not always evaluate the same advertisements, the results of comparing combination E with combination C or D are indeterminate. Although the state regulation was sporadic, it was significant enough to discourage many advertisers from making claims, even if they had not been subject to state scrutiny. Nevertheless, combination E can be preferable to combination D and perhaps even to combination C. Such a case would occur with a large advertiser with an innovative campaign who asks the regulator applying the correct standard to approve his ad. If that approval has the effect of discouraging or at least tempering the regulators applying the incorrect standard, then multiple regulators applying different standards (combination E) could conceivably, at least for that product, produce a better result for consumers than in the cases where one (combination C) or many (combination D) regulators applied an incorrect standard. In essence this is what Kellogg did when it secured the cooperation of the National Cancer

---

[19]This conclusion treats the NLEA as having a single enforcer, although it in fact allows for state enforcement. The "right of first refusal" for FDA should reduce, although it may not eliminate, the substantive costs resulting from the most restrictive judgment. To the extent the states are active, combination D is a more accurate description of the result.

Institute to defy the FDA's prohibition on health claims. (Kellogg's strategy was no doubt aided by the fact that the NCI and the FDA are part of the same federal agency.)

Although the states did not attack the Kellogg campaign, in most cases when the two evaluated the same claims, the states were unwilling to defer to the FTC. Because of the uncertainty resulting from state regulation and the additional uncertainty from the FDA's still-evolving regulations, many in the advertising community supported national regulation. As we saw in the previous section, many businesses prefer certainty and uniformity, with its reduction in cost, even if the resulting standard harms consumers. The relevant issue is whether, given the compromise necessary to achieve uniformity, the NLEA on balance harmed consumers.

In answering this question, at least three points are relevant. First, if the "vacuum" caused by the absence of the NLEA deterred truthful claims that the act permits, then the federal statute offers a significant benefit. Yet to reach this conclusion one would have to decide either that the NLEA resulted in a better standard than that applied by the states, whose more restrictive standard governed most pre-NLEA claims, or that it was not possible to determine what standard the states were applying.

Regarding the states' standard, although they supported an FDA ban, they did not attack all health claims. In particular, they did not attack the claims linking fiber with cancer, which the FDA proposes to prohibit. Moreover, an advertiser wishing to make a claim could have negotiated with the states about its contents.[20] The argument that the absence of the NLEA deterred more claims than the act itself is correct only if it was impossible or so difficult to determine the states' standards that a de facto ban on health claims resulted. Given the willingness of the states to discuss claims with advertisers and the fact that many claims went unchallenged, this point seems dubious at best.

Ultimately, the impact of the NLEA on consumers will depend upon the substantive position of the FDA. We have seen that the

---

[20]There is, however, a public good aspect to such an effort by an individual advertiser. Once one company has developed an acceptable campaign, competitors can initiate the claim at much lower cost. Although this problem reduces the incentive to make the effort, some companies may well have done so, as Kellogg did at the federal level.

FDA's position is restrictive indeed. To the extent that legislation results applying the NLEA to advertising, the result will be even worse. In any event, many advertisers will feel constrained to follow FDA rules regarding advertising regardless of the FTC's views, given the FDA's proclivity to determine that health claims make a food a drug and thus subject to FDA jurisdiction. Moreover, food manufacturers now frequently make products (such as fat substitutes) that require FDA approval to market, and hence they will be less willing to defy the FDA than in an era when they had less need for its blessing.

A second argument in favor of the NLEA is that the states will defer to any clear federal standard, resulting in a situation like that in combination C. Yet the two cases in which the states are most likely to defer do not necessarily benefit consumers. In one, the states will defer to a standard that prohibits most useful information, as does the currently proposed FDA regulation. In such a case, consumers can find little solace in the retreat of the states, for there is little left for the states to do. Business will have achieved uniformity, with its resulting reduction in procedural cost, only at a high price to consumers. In the other case, the states are likely to defer to specific and detailed standards, such as the FDA has proposed for nutritional labeling. Whether consumers will benefit depends, once again, on the substantive merits of the standards. The more judgmental the standard—such as prohibitions on "misleading" statements—the less likely it is that deference will follow.

A third justification raised for the NLEA is that either a federal statute or a regulation was bound to exist, and any federal standard would have been highly restrictive regarding health claims. Even if true, there are sound reasons to have preferred discretionary FDA regulation to that mandated by statute. Discretionary regulation can be changed more easily than can a statute. Moreover, the White House, which is more sympathetic than the Congress to the consumer-oriented arguments of the FTC, would have had more influence on discretionary regulation. Finally, regulation could have more clearly delineated FTC-FDA responsibilities, mitigating against the current effort to require the FTC to apply FDA labeling rules to advertising.

Of course, this view that regulation was preferable to a statute was relevant only if business opposition, combined with FDA regula-

131

tion, could have prevented passage of the statute. Both authors, with experience at the FTC and the OMB, believed this was the case, although the point is now moot. In any event, proponents of the NLEA argue that it was preferable to FDA regulation because the FDA was unwilling to preempt. Yet the NLEA did not provide the preemption the business community desired the most—that of California's Proposition 65, which may require health warnings on food labels. Moreover, the NLEA's preemption does not in fact prevent the states from challenging health claims. Proponents of the NLEA respond that the detailed nature of the FDA's regulation under the NLEA and the requirement that the states discuss matters with the FDA before suing will effectively result in state deference to the FDA. There is force in these arguments. But these results could have been obtained under a regulatory approach, even without direct preemption.

Thus, the NLEA is the worst of all possible worlds. Compared with the scenario of no detailed federal regulations, the interplay among agencies exemplified by combination E and the Kellogg example was preferable. Even if regulation was bound to occur, FDA regulation alone, as opposed to the less flexible federal legislation and the FDA's implementing rules, would in the long run have been more beneficial to consumers.

Multiple Regulators—Conclusion

Many of the usual arguments for federalism do not apply to state regulation of national advertising. The costs of adapting campaigns to individual jurisdictions are sufficiently high that the outcome of significant state regulation is a national standard. The issue is not whether different decisions should be permitted at the state level, but whether national decisions should be made by individual states.

Even with a single correct standard, multiple regulators impose significant costs. Substantive costs result because the most restrictive judgment, rather than the most accurate, will prevail. Procedural costs are increased as well. Multiple enforcers of a uniform but incorrect standard are more costly still, because the most restrictive judgment tightens the regulatory ratchet even further.

To avoid excessive procedural costs, businesses facing multiple regulators have generally argued for a single standard. To achieve

132

uniformity, however, compromise is necessary, which results in an overly restrictive standard. For businesses, the direct procedural cost savings may well be sufficient to make this solution attractive, especially as companies may not face the full costs of the incorrect standard. The best outcome for consumers, however, is far more sensitive to the substance of the standard that actually results. The procedural costs of multiple regulators, along with the tightening that results from the most restrictive judgment, may well be less than the costs of an incorrect standard. At least for health claims, where the drama is largely over, a uniform federal statute appears to be the worst result for consumers.

8
Bureaucratic Influences

GOVERNMENT AGENCIES are not run by philosopher kings who descend from Olympus to protect us. Instead, these agencies are governed by rules that constrain what they can do, and by individuals who are striving for advancement, as we all are. The following section discusses the differences in the constraints and incentives facing the states and the FTC and the importance of those differences. Then, we briefly consider two other issues: the effects of the divergence between business and consumer interests, and the relevance of a second federal regulator, the FDA for health claims and the EPA for environmental claims.

Differences between the FTC and the States

There are important differences between the FTC and the states. For one, even though its staff was reduced significantly over the past decade, the FTC has significantly more resources than have individual states. Second, most attorneys general are elected, and they are often running for higher office. Conversely, those at the FTC seek advancement not through election, but in the bar or in higher government jobs. Third, FTC commissioners are intimately involved in making both antitrust and consumer protection decisions. Indeed, many more of them come to the commission with a background in antitrust than in consumer protection, and it is primarily to antitrust that most of them return when they leave the commission. Attorneys general are not experts in either antitrust or consumer protection. Although they routinely supervise both functions, they have many other duties as well. Hence they delegate more and are less involved in detailed analyses of the issues than are the decision makers at the FTC. These characterizations do not describe every action by every employee, but they hold true for a significant body of the regulators.

134

What are the consequences of these differences? One is that the states will use simple theories more often than will the federal government, because the states do not have the resources to do otherwise. This difference helps explain the states' reluctance to retreat from the fools test and their avoidance of the modern FTC reliance on consumer surveys and other sophisticated evidence for determining the meaning of an advertisement.[1] Attorneys representing businesses in state investigations say the states have repeatedly indicated an inability to conduct consumer surveys and, in some cases, have even been unwilling to consider surveys conducted by others.

A second difference involves financing. State involvement with national advertising has so far been self-financed. States have obtained cash payments as part of most settlements, which to the extent that state law allows have provided resources for the next cases. In the current budget crisis of many states, the attorneys general are even more dependent upon self-financing. This fact has at least two consequences. First, unlike the FTC, the states cannot afford many "dry holes" from their investigations. Second, the need for settlement produces relatively weak orders, as we discuss more fully below.

Another difference in the states' greater tendency to seek highly visible cases. Was it a coincidence that when some states chose to sue national retailers for deceptive pricing, those suits were filed at the height of the Christmas shopping season?[2] Moreover, the states are now concerned about the so-called downsizing of packages, a highly visible issue that the Federal Trade Commission at the height of its activism in the 1970s decided to ignore. The FTC is hardly opposed to visibility. All else equal it would love a visible case, but it is more likely than the states to develop a complex body of law. The FTC has more resources to do so, and developing and administering that body of law is useful in gaining the knowledge that helps the careers of those at the commission.

A striking example of this difference in visibility is the contrast in the rhetoric used by the FTC and by the officials of some states. FTC commissioners, who will sit as judges to decide the issues in

---

[1] We characterize the fools test as a simple theory because it is easy to use in court, avoiding the need for extrinsic evidence.

[2] In late 1989, New York sued Sears and North Carolina sued J.C. Penney.

the cases they bring, are loathe to engage in excessive rhetoric about individual cases.[3] Moreover, the commissioners' interest in preserving their own freedom to make decisions leads to rules and internal incentives that prevent the staff who prosecute the cases from discussing the matter publicly, particularly before the commission has decided to issue a complaint. Colorful rhetoric would create pressure for commission action, which would effectively shift more decision-making authority to the staff.

The states do not feel so constrained. The attorney general in charge of the state's environmental task force proclaimed that after they had finished cleaning up the health claim scams ("the cholesterol craze"), they were moving next to the potentially greater problems involving environmental claims.[4] The FTC rarely employs strident rhetoric, even when it is pursuing hard-core frauds. National advertisers are not used to having their claims so characterized, and are most wary of the resulting publicity. The rhetoric is not surprising, however, given the states' desire for visibility and the simplicity of their policy: that is, all health claims should be prohibited. Rhetoric can help achieve that objective. Moreover, intemperate rhetoric directed at an out-of-state company is unlikely to produce an effective political response.

An even more striking example of inflamed rhetoric is that of Texas's former assistant attorney general, Stephen Gardner. He proclaimed that one product claiming to be fat-free is "not fat-free; it is truth-free."[5] Mr. Gardner made this claim even though he was still investigating the product and had yet to file suit. Although he was not representative of all assistant attorneys general, companies could not ignore him because he came from a large state. Officials in other large states defended him, at least publicly. A lawyer who ran the New York Consumer Protection Bureau stated that public lawyers must keep the public informed through the media, and that "there

---

[3]In rule making, colorful rhetoric can provoke congressional oversight and restrictions on the agency. The staff's rhetorical excesses, which Michael Pertschuk characterized as reflecting a "vendetta," figured prominently in congressional restrictions on the FTC's funeral rule.

[4]See Scott Hume, "State Attorney General Issues 'Green' Warning," *Advertising Age* (November 13, 1989), p. 3.

[5]Christi Harlan, "Texas Law Official Stirs Up Marketers," *The Wall Street Journal*, June 6, 1991.

are times when being vocal is important for the case you are involved in and for the public."[6]

Mr. Gardner's boss, who like many attorneys general sought higher office, was fully supportive. Although the attorney general lost his campaign for governor and although he noted that Mr. Gardner made powerful enemies for him, he said his assistant "did exactly what I wanted him to do."[7] Supporters claim that what the attorney general wanted done was to attack fraud and deception; critics maintain his motive can be summarized in one word: publicity.

A third difference between the states and the FTC is that the states are more reluctant to risk litigation. Litigation is expensive, with little payoff in visibility. But at the FTC, litigation provides both experience for attorneys and a forum for developing a complex body of law.[8] The state experience with litigation in consumer protection

---

[6]Ibid.

[7]Ibid.

[8]One might ask why, if the attorney general delegates to his staff, the staff does not have the same incentives as the FTC staff to develop a complex body of law. One answer is that the FTC consumer protection staff, to the extent it only does consumer protection, has limited incentives, relative to top officials, to develop such a body of law. There are few private jobs that predominately involve consumer protection. Most private attorneys spend a majority of their time elsewhere, particularly in antitrust. The result is that those who run the FTC, the commissioners and bureau directors, view consumer protection as a complement to their antitrust knowledge. These top officials will likely practice some consumer protection when they leave the agency, and thus have more incentive than the lower staff to prefer that the law be complex. A similar phenomena has not yet developed at the state level.

In any event, another reason for the difference in incentives is the forum in which cases are tried. FTC cases are tried before administrative law judges, who themselves accumulate considerable experience and knowledge about advertising regulation. State cases are tried in state courts, before judges who have usually not seen an advertising case before. Simple theories are more likely to succeed, and the paucity of precedent under most state statutes means there is little need to develop complex distinctions from prior cases.

Although most state statutes give some status to FTC cases as precedents, the sizable number of cases and the evolution of the commission's approach to advertising means that it is possible to find some precedent for nearly anything. As discussed in part one, state activity is often based on theories that the FTC abandoned long ago. While the FTC focuses on the more recent cases and approaches in developing its theories, the states have focused on older cases. Nonetheless, there is FTC precedent for both theories. In the absence of state cases, it is unclear which precedents a particular state court will follow.

has not been favorable. In the *May D & F* case, for example—the major, recent example of a fully litigated, large-scale consumer protection case undertaken by a state—Colorado sued May for deceptive pricing.[9] The state spent huge sums on the case, failed to obtain the injunctive relief it sought, and won only nominal damages for consumers. Although the court did award the state money for costs, the amount was far less than the state claimed it had spent. Moreover, in the 1990 election, the opponent of the attorney general who had filed the case used the attorney general's failures against the May Company in an advertisement. Whatever the impact of the ad, the incumbent lost.

Another example involves the litigation against Mobil. As discussed earlier, several states sued Mobil on somewhat different grounds regarding Mobil's environmental claims for its Hefty trash bags. The case was a quagmire for the states, because it involved complicated issues of science and of consumer perception. The states do not have the resources to engage systematically in such litigation.

At the FTC such litigation, although not the common method of resolving cases, occurs much more frequently. Because of the unwillingness to litigate and the greater emphasis on visibility, compared with the Federal Trade Commission, the states issue weak orders. Many of the states' most publicized efforts for example, are merely assurances of voluntary compliance. Although the states ultimately settled the case with Mobil, the Stipulated Settlement Orders were quite favorable to Mobil.[10]

We are not suggesting that additional resources would solve the problems of the states. Given the incentives of the attorneys general for higher elected office and the problems of litigating before state judges, such an increase would probably only exacerbate the problem. Furthermore, adding more money would not address the final

---

The simplicity of state theories and their roots in abandoned FTC precedents may not survive state litigation. That, of course, is part of the reason why states are more reluctant to risk litigation.

[9]Colorado v. the May Department Store d/b/a May D & F, case no. 90 CA 1795 (1990).

[10]Unlike the typical FTC order, the states placed no restrictions on Mobil's future conduct. Nevertheless, from Mobil's standpoint, although it was better equipped to deal with the complicated issues, litigation was quite expensive, itself a significant incentive to settle the cases.

and perhaps most important difference between the states and the FTC: the role of antitrust at the Federal Trade Commission.

Antitrust permeates what the FTC does. The antitrust philosophy, which itself has evolved significantly over the past twenty years, is market-oriented in that its theoretical underpinnings are based on consumer sovereignty and freely functioning markets. The importance of antitrust has led those at the FTC to view advertising regulation in a similar manner—as an attempt to make the market work better, not as an effort to supplant consumer decision making. As a result, arguments for regulating health claims based on the "appropriate" diet, like environmental claims based on the "appropriate" environmental policy, are inconsistent with the commissioners' basic approach.[11] As we noted above, many attorneys general do not review matters as closely as do federal trade commissioners.[12]

These differences between the FTC and the states have important implications for the future of national advertising. In both health and environmental claims, the current political trend is not toward eliminating the states' role in enforcement, but instead toward devising uniform standards that the states could enforce for these claims. This is the approach of the recent Nutrition Labeling and Education Act, and it would be the result of FTC guidelines on environmental claims.[13] As explained in chapter 7, however, even uniform standards

[11]It is true that the FTC staff that does consumer protection is not as imbued in this antitrust ethic as the commissioners. Although the staff exerts powerful influences over the commissioners through the investigations it pursues and the information it generates, the commissioners, who are the final decision makers, ultimately determine the questions the staff must address. Moreover, economists are much more involved in consumer protection at the FTC than at the state level. The importance of antitrust in checking consumer protection is one reason why many believe that the FTC should retain its current structure, rather than transferring the antitrust function to the Department of Justice. See 1989 ABA Report, pp. 109–10.

[12]There is another difference between the constraints facing antitrust and consumer protection that is worth noting. The courts are an increasingly important constraint in antitrust. In consumer protection, that constraint is much less relevant, giving the FTC more freedom to act. At the Federal Trade Commission, for example, when a court overturns the agency in an advertising case it is usually because the order was too strenuous or because the commission did not have jurisdiction; it is not because the court disagreed about the substantive violation that the commission found.

[13]The guidelines would create uniform standards in the sense that the states have

will result in a significant change in advertising, given the presence of multiple regulators. The differences in the constraints and incentives between the FTC and the states virtually guarantee that different judgments will be applied when using the same standards. Thus, as long as the states remain active, the result will be a decrease in the quantity of valuable information flowing to consumers, regardless of the uniform standards applied.

We do not conclude that the states will remain as strident as they were in the late 1980s. Indeed, we discuss below their willingness to compromise with the Federal Trade Commission. In late 1991 Stephen Gardner was asked to leave his post as assistant attorney general of Texas—a step that may indicate a movement at least toward moderation of rhetoric.[14]

The continued presence of the states in this issue may influence the substance of the ultimate standards adopted, or at least their application by the FTC. The states criticized the FTC for "abandoning enforcement" during the 1980s.[15] In the 1990s, the FTC has worked much more closely with the states. At least both sides have stopped publicly criticizing each other. To the extent this attitude results in a desire to compromise with the states, it will require some change in principle. Indeed, one major cooperative effort of the states and the FTC to date resulted in such a compromise.[16]

---

expressed a desire to follow them, and because virtually every state has a "little FTC act" that requires some level of deference to the pronouncements of the national FTC.

[14]Initially Mr. Gardner's new boss was supportive. A spokesman stated, "Gardner has a national reputation now for being a very aggressive consumer advocate and he has the go-ahead from the attorney general. He pretty much has free reign." See Harlan, "Texas Law Official."

[15]Like most others who try to explain various regulatory phenomena, we have no clear idea why the states became aggressive at the time they did, although the FTC's evolution away from the theories of the 1960s did create an opportunity that had not previously existed. As we discuss below, the FTC and the states are attempting to reconcile their views, but we doubt that the states will abandon the field entirely. Moreover, as indicated in the discussion in chapter 6 of the *Green Reports*, the views that the states have most recently espoused still reflect considerable variance from modern FTC regulation of advertising. Their comments urging the FDA to tighten its already strict regulations under the NLEA support the same conclusion.

[16]The FTC and state settlements regarding Bunnies also indicate compromise on the part of the FTC, as discussed in chapter 6.

The case involved two advertisements, one of which showed an uncooked and a cooked chicken leg and read, "Add Mazola, reduce cholesterol." If consumers interpreted the ad as comparing chicken cooked in Mazola with chicken cooked in something else, the ad was in fact true. But the FTC interpreted the ad as implying that even an increased total consumption of fried chicken would reduce the consumer's cholesterol count. Commissioner Terry Calvani dissented, fearing a return to the FTC's more militant policy of the 1960s. Because the commission's interpretation of the ad is not utterly implausible, Calvani's dissent is an overreaction, although the failure to copy test the ad is hard to justify. Some states challenged other Mazola ads but abandoned their call for a prohibition on health claims at least for this case. Thus both sides retreated from previous positions.[17]

If extensive state involvement with regulation of national advertising continues, mechanisms have to be developed to reduce the costs to consumers. Cooperative investigations against fraud and state assistance in enforcing certain FTC rules are steps in the right direction. Such cases are far less prone to differences in judgment than the typical national advertising case. Fraud cases generally involve clear-cut violations, with express claims that are false. Rules such as the one for used cars have specific requirements.

One possible solution in the broader realm of advertising regulation would be to authorize states to bring such cases either in federal court or in a proceeding before the FTC.[18] Either approach would probably ensure a single standard, and either would reduce the problem of having the most restrictive judgment govern national

[17]There is another difference between the states and the FTC that may encourage the FTC to become more active. Congress, with its large staffs and long sessions, exerts more influence on the FTC than do the legislatures of some states, who have relatively smaller staffs and are not as intrusive with regulatory agencies. When the political environment in Congress encourages intervention, the FTC will be more active than it would otherwise be, all else equal. These issues are complex, and one of the authors has explored them elsewhere. See Timothy J. Muris, "Regulatory Policy Making at the Federal Trade Commission: The Extent of Congressional Control," *Journal of Political Economy*, vol. 94 (1986), p. 884.

[18]Such a scheme should also confine the states to the remedies available to the FTC—a cease and desist order, and restitution in cases of fraudulent and dishonest conduct. Unlike current state proceedings, cases under this approach would not be self-financing.

advertising. Proceedings before the FTC would make the commission's judgments prevail. In the federal courts, precedent would develop a more consistent standard, and the courts' likely insistence on evidence of an advertisement's meaning would greatly reduce the problem of having the most restrictive judgment prevail. Under the Lanham Act, for example, and in cases tried by the FTC in federal court, courts have insisted on survey evidence when the meaning of an advertisement is in doubt.[19] Indeed, the development of a body of judicial precedent on the meaning of the prohibition on deceptive practices could serve as a valuable check on the commission as well.

A federal right of action for state attorneys general, however, is not ideal. As we have noted, most cases are resolved through consent agreements, because the value of a particular advertising claim is often not worth the costs of litigation and the additional adverse publicity. When an advertiser is unwilling to litigate, the most restrictive judgment will still prevail in a settlement. Moreover, to solve the problems of multiple enforcers, a federal proceeding would have to be the states' only remedy against advertising that involved interstate commerce. Without such preemption, states could choose to proceed instead under state statutes, creating the same difficulties as the present system.

Divergence in Business and Consumer Interests

When multiple regulators apply multiple standards, firms face the costs of dealing with the states, even if they would have prevailed under federal standards. These procedural costs of dealing with multiple standards may be high and are reflected in product costs. For consumers, having a uniform substantive regulation that discourages appropriate advertising may be less desirable than having multiple standards, despite the procedural costs of such duplication. When the FTC and the states are speaking to each other, as is

---

[19]A major FTC case tried in federal court, instead of in an administrative proceeding, was FTC v. Brown & Williamson (D.C. Cir 1985), involving claims that the Barclay cigarettes had one milligram of tar. Although the FTC also challenged claims that Barclay was "99 percent tar-free," the district court judge dismissed that count, because survey evidence did not support the commission's interpretation of the claim. See FTC v. Brown & Williamson 580 F.Supp. 981 (D.D.C. 1983).

currently the case, a clever business may be able to use the FTC and its standards to produce an ad campaign that survives the states' scrutiny unscathed. When the procedural costs are not prohibitive, consumers as a group may be willing to pay them rather than face a bad substantive standard.

It is not clear that businesses face the same incentives. Consider a product with a nutrition advantage. Although consumers want that information to be communicated, competitors do not, if they lack the advantage. Moreover, many businesses will have great difficulty identifying their likely success in competition based on dimensions different from those currently used, as for example with health versus taste. They may be willing to accept a uniform set of federal rules that create a more stable regulatory environment, even if it deters innovation.

This argument may explain why many businesses so eagerly supported the labeling statute, despite its obvious restrictions on information. At least some business support may also have resulted from a difference between the costs facing large and small businesses. Scale economies exist with regulation. Many larger firms have in-house legal specialists to handle complicated regulations. Similarly, if significant innovations are more likely to come from smaller firms, larger firms would on average prefer a uniform standard that deterred innovation.

The public-goods nature of much information also results in some divergence between the interests of businesses and of consumers. Claims about the benefits of high-fiber diets in reducing the risk of cancer, for example, produce benefits for all producers of high-fiber products. Only the company that makes the claim bears the costs, however. Thus the benefit of the claim to consumers is generally greater than the benefit to the company that makes it. As a result, businesses are more willing than consumers to agree to restricting such claims.

The Presence of a Second Federal Regulator

The presence of a second federal regulator creates another complication. In health, the FDA and the FTC have jurisdiction, the former scrutinizing claims on labels and the latter focusing on claims in media advertising. Although this division of labor is formalized in an

143

interagency agreement, each can scrutinize either form of communication.[20] For environmental claims, the EPA appears to desire a role.

The Federal Trade Commission examines advertisements for the messages they provide consumers, seeking to determine accuracy. To both the FDA and the EPA, this policy is of little concern; instead, the FDA considers the "appropriate" diet for the public from the standpoint of health and the EPA considers the "appropriate" environmental policy, as for example in waste disposal. Although the role of consumer sovereignty in meeting these policies should be central to the FDA and the EPA, it is not. Neither agency is permeated with the market-oriented philosophy of antitrust. Indeed, each agency was established to replace market activities with a congressionally mandated solution, and neither has shown much inclination to limit its intervention to situations resulting from the market failure that justifies its existence.

Furthermore, significant differences between the FTC and the other agencies characterize the incentive structures and professional backgrounds of regulators. The FTC's primary operation is law enforcement, with the usual presumption that conduct is acceptable until proven otherwise. The FDA, in contrast, is predominantly a "gatekeeper" agency, charged with deciding which products can be permitted to enter the marketplace. Its usual presumption is that products cannot be sold until proved safe.

Erroneous decisions to approve a product generate high costs for the agency and presumably for the responsible employees, but erroneous decisions to reject a product are virtually invisible. Indeed, the FDA is famous for its reluctance in the new drug approval process to recognize that refusal to approve a product can also create safety risks. The costs to consumers may be enormous, but at least until the AIDS crisis, the political cost to the agency was nonexistent. At the FTC, in contrast, the costs of erroneous decisions are more symmetric. Depending on the fit between its policies and the prevailing political climate, the FTC has been sharply criticized both for failure to act against perceived deceptive practices and for inappropriate action against desirable practices.

The FDA is also a scientific agency, with a strong bias in favor of delaying a decision until conclusive evidence is available. For the FDA's many scientists, remaining uncommitted about a particular

---

[20]*Federal Register*, vol. 36 (1971), p. 18,539.

hypothesis until the definitive study is conducted is normal professional behavior. Their interest lies more in the scientific question—
for example, Is the hypothesis that dietary fiber reduces the cancer
risk correct? than in the policy question—Should we permit such
claims? The lawyers and economists at the FTC, in contrast, are
trained to make policy decisions in the face of incomplete information. Indeed, a persistent criticism of the FTC is that the commission
is too willing to act without adequate evidence.[21]

There are undeniably important differences between labels and
advertisements, and the FTC has used them in the past to allow more
flexibility than was permitted under FDA rules. But the new statute
and FDA regulations under it will certainly influence the FTC, even
if the Moakley bill discussed in chapter 5 is not enacted. To avoid
obvious conflicts, the FTC will probably defer to FDA definitions of
product-description terms such as "light," although the FTC may try
to influence the FDA's determination. Similarly, the FTC is likely to
follow an FDA conclusion that a particular health claim is not
supported by adequate scientific evidence, much as it has followed—
sometimes blindly—the FDA's requirement of two clinical studies to
support drug-efficacy claims. When the FDA is studying an issue,
however, the FTC will probably feel less constrained and more willing
to permit claims without the extreme disclosure the FDA seeks.

The FDA's enhanced role through the NLEA and the potential
for those standards to be congressionally applied to advertising may
have influenced the FTC's October 1991 complaint against Stouffer.
The advertisement claimed that Lean Cuisine entrees contained "less
than 1 gram of sodium*." One FTC theory appears largely factual:
namely, that in many cases when the advertisement was dissemi-
nated, Lean Cuisine was not low in sodium. A second allegation,
however, appears dubious. The FTC charges that the advertising has
"failed" to disclose adequately that 1 gram is equivalent to 1,000
milligrams, "which is the commonly used measurement for sodium."

Yet the advertisement itself disclosed, in the footnote to which
the "*" after "sodium" referred, that 1 gram equaled "1,000 mg."
The disclosure is prominent, it is only about one-half inch from the
textual statement that it qualifies, and it is separated from that textual

---

[21]See for example, Timothy J. Muris, "Rules without Reason," *Regulation*, vol. 6
(September/October 1982), p. 20.

statement by only a few words of advertising copy. Given this apparent adequacy of the disclosure, it may be that the FTC was influenced by a desire to stop the Moakley bill. Indeed, in his statement introducing the legislation, Congressman Moakley discussed the precise issue of the Stouffer ad:

> Food advertising may also use some measurement units which are not allowed by FDA for labeling purposes. An example would be using a claim of less than one gram of salt, which may imply a product which is low in sodium. FDA requires that sodium be listed in milligram units.[22]

In any event, the FTC's ultimate reaction may depend upon whether it feels it has supporters, particularly in the business community. Without such support, the FTC's ability and interest in deviating from the FDA will decrease. Because many businesses have reasons to oppose the FTC's modern view of advertising regulation as applied to health and environmental claims, such support will not be automatic.

Bureaucratic Influences—Conclusion

We have not attempted to explain fully why the FTC and the states act as they do. We do say that the differences between them are relevant to any explanation of their differences in behavior. Given the nature of bureaucratic and political institutions, the continued presence of the states, the FTC, and the FDA as regulators of national advertising and labeling campaigns will result in some compromises. In fact, the FTC appears to be responding to both the states and the FDA. Finally, because of the differences between consumer and business interests, the business community is unlikely to support automatically the regulatory principles the FTC has devised in the past two decades. Such a failure of support will itself increase the pressure for the FTC to deviate from its regulatory principles.

---

[22]*Congressional Record*, April 9, 1991, p. E 1,165.

9

Conclusion

NATIONAL FIRMS apply the standards of the agency that Congress charged with regulating national advertising—the Federal Trade Commission. Since the 1970s in particular, most national advertisers have successfully incorporated the FTC's concerns in their compliance programs. Yet in recent years these firms have had to do more than apply the rules of the national regulatory body. State activities have produced a multiplicity of advertising regulators and standards, creating serious problems, because even responsible regulators using identical standards may disagree in close cases.

Business leaders and many others have emphasized uniform standards, but not the displacement of the states as regulators. Even with optimal regulatory standards, optimally enforced at the federal level, the presence of multiple regulators results in less than an optimal amount of information flowing to consumers. In their efforts to comply with differing interpretations of multiple regulations, companies that attempt to advertise nationally are effectively governed by the most restrictive view that any significant regulator decides to take.

Thus the "federalism" arguments frequently made to justify state and local regulation do not apply. State regulation of national advertising necessarily transcends its own borders. If the states are wrong—and we have seen that, compared with the Federal Trade Commission, state regulators are likely to be overly restrictive—the costs are imposed on consumers nationwide. Because of the nature of national advertising and the impact of state regulation, there can be no laboratory to evaluate competing forms of regulation. Except in small states, state regulation displaces that of the central government when it is more restrictive.

Matters are further complicated because state regulators do not all apply the same legal standards to evaluate advertising. At the

147

federal level, there is a strong consensus about the standards that should be employed in advertising regulation, but that consensus is threatened. The threat comes not from the emergence of new ideas about how advertising should be regulated, but from the emergence of new state regulators who have not learned the lessons of the commission's experience. The resulting substantive differences between the standards used by federal and state regulators, and the differences among state regulators, create additional problems. To avoid prosecution, national advertising must comply with the most restrictive standard that any significant state chooses to employ.

Beginning in the 1970s, federal trade commissioners of all political persuasions have believed that advertising is an important element of effective competition. Consumers need information about product alternatives if their choices are to guide a market economy, and advertising provides that information. It stimulates product innovation and encourages manufacturers to introduce products that better serve consumers' needs. The FTC's recent Bureau of Economics study of health claims for high-fiber cereals documents these important market effects. The study found that after health claims began, new product introductions increased, as did the weighted-average fiber content of cereals. Because competition occurs in national markets, state or local activity that impairs the use of truthful advertising as a competitive tool threatens those benefits to consumers in other jurisdictions. The present regulatory cacophony threatens the contribution of truthful advertising to the benefits that vigorous competition offers to consumers.

Moreover, the commission has reached a broad consensus that regulators should not pursue advertising claims that are not material to consumers, or that are deceptive only when subject to bizarre or idiosyncratic interpretations. When regulators act against advertising that truthfully informs the overwhelming majority because a small and unrepresentative minority might misinterpret the message, they deny valuable information to the majority. Yet some state actions are based on the standard that advertising is prohibited even if only "wayfaring men, though fools," might be misled.

Even when national standards have been drafted in recent years, the states appear to have influenced the outcome. Although some differences exist between ads and labels, a proconsumer position would encourage truthful health claims on both. Yet some states, applying the outdated principles they apply to advertising, would ban such claims. The latest congressional approach, more sensitive to the ability of the marketplace to educate and benefit consumers, would allow some claims. But with its many restrictions, this approach is flawed.

The problem with the congressional approach is its attempt to determine in advance which claims are "suitable" for food labels. In reality, any information that is truthful and not misleading should be suitable—on labels, in advertising, or elsewhere—as long as consumers find it useful. The valid gauge of usefulness is the marketplace, not the opinion of a government committee. The FDA should police health messages to ensure they are truthful and not misleading, but it should not be the arbiter deciding which truths are suitable for consumers to hear.

The compromise in the federal statute on labels between the FTC's and the states' positions has left the FTC in a difficult posture regarding advertising. Historically it has largely ignored FDA principles in evaluating health claims in advertising, but the FTC is under increasing pressure to conform. Many in the business community approve of the FTC's standards for evaluating advertising, but their views are not unanimous. Business and consumer interests diverge significantly regarding regulation of advertising. It is the innovators who benefit most from the modern FTC's views and not all firms are innovators. Moreover, businesses bear the procedural costs of multiple regulation, but they do not bear all the substantive costs of suboptimal regulatory standards or their enforcement.[1]

It is not clear whether the health claims story will be repeated for environmental claims. Significant similarities exist. Some states, using policy preferences based on their views of environmental policy rather than on regulation of advertising, seek to retard environmental advertising significantly. Another federal agency, the EPA, is concerned over the claims at issue. The FTC, with little experience in applying its advertising policy to environmental claims, is under substantial pressure to compromise.

There are also important differences from health claims. The states have been less aggressive, and since their initial involvement

---

[1]Of course, they can raise prices to reflect those costs. Increased prices, however, result in a decrease in consumer purchases.

149

they have called for uniform federal standards, drafted by the FTC. The EPA lacks the history of the FDA in dealing with health claims. The FTC, with the pen in its hand, has an opportunity to shape standards closer to the optimal than are those regarding health claims on labels. Moreover, the FTC's efforts in the past two years to assuage the states represent both an opportunity and a danger: an opportunity because the improved relations should increase the deference of the states to FTC guidelines, and a danger because, to the extent the FTC feels the necessity of compromise, the standards will necessarily retreat from those dictated by the modern FTC approach to advertising.

Environmental advertising guides based on the principles of advertising regulation would recognize that context is critical. They would not attempt to impose a one-word, one-meaning approach. Through the general requirement that claims must be substantiated, they would allow and probably encourage claims based on the latest and most reliable scientific methodologies, even if those methodologies have not been reduced to a precise cookbook recipe. Guides based on advertising policy would seek to ensure that consumers get what they bargain for, without first determining whether that is the ideal environmental policy. Thus claims of recyclability or compostability would be viewed as pertaining to capability, rather than likelihood. They would avoid creating artificial distinctions among materials based on the regulator's own notion of how best to rearrange the world. And they would recognize that vague but appealing language such as "environmentally friendly" or "green" can have an important role in attracting and holding the consumer's attention sufficiently to convey a more specific message.

In sum, advertising regulation concerns the national economy. National advertising transcends state and local borders, and any significant regulation, be it from the federal government, a large state, or a group of states, has a nationwide impact. Thus, deference to the states has little justification in this important area of our economy.

150